RUSSIA ⊠ TRANSITION

ECOLOGICAL DISASTER

CLEANING UP THE HIDDEN LEGACY OF THE SOVIET REGIME

MURRAY FESHBACH

A TWENTIETH CENTURY FUND REPORT

ECOLOGICAL DISASTER

ECOLOGICAL DISASTER

CLEANING UP THE HIDDEN LEGACY OF THE SOVIET REGIME

MURRAY FESHBACH

A TWENTIETH CENTURY FUND REPORT

The Twentieth Century Fund Press ◆ New York ◆ 1995

The Twentieth Century Fund sponsors and supervises timely analyses of economic policy, foreign affairs, and domestic political issues. Not-for-profit and nonpartisan, the Fund was founded in 1919 and endowed by Edward A. Filene.

Library of Congress Cataloging-in-Publication Data

Feshbach, Murray, 1929–
  Ecological disaster: cleaning up the hidden legacy of the Soviet regime / Murray Feshbach.
      p. cm.
  "A Twentieth century fund report."
  Includes bibliographical references and index.
  ISBN 0-87078-364-5
  1. Environmental health--Russia (Federation). 2. Environmental degradation--Russia (Federations). I. Title.
  RA566.5.R9F47 1995
  363.7 '00947--dc20   94–41853

                                                                CIP

Cover Design: Claude Goodwin
Manufactured in the United States of America.

FOREWORD

During the course of the cold war, the United States committed immense resources to the task of penetrating the veil of secrecy surrounding its great adversary, the Soviet Union. Guesswork—sometimes educated, sometimes not—was a major component of Western estimates of the basic facts about the USSR's economy, natural resources, military, government, and everyday affairs. The final proof, however, that the essence of Soviet internal affairs eluded us until the end was the overwhelming shock of the sudden reversal of past belligerency and the subsequent rapid breakup of the Communist empire.

Given the new, breathtakingly more open societies of the former Soviet Union, we can expect to and do know much more about almost every facet of life. In fact, the information that has gradually emerged since 1989 is dispelling many false presumptions, adding depth to our previously sketchy notions. But, today's greater accessibility does not mean that we have suddenly entered an era of crystal clarity. To the contrary, old habits die hard; and many remnants of Soviet officialdom and media still produce information and statistics that fall far short of contemporary American standards for accuracy.

Still, some experts have worked hard to piece together a sharper picture of current conditions in the former Soviet bloc. In the area of environmental concerns, Murray Feshbach's work has received special attention. In this paper, he builds on the work that went into the widely admired book he coauthored in 1992 with Alfred Friendly, Jr., *Ecocide in the USSR*. Indeed, the fact that great uncertainty persists about Russian environmental problems makes the continuing work of Feshbach and others especially important. They are engaged in the difficult task of discovering the true magnitude of the widespread environmental degradation that was so routinely a part of Soviet economic activity.

In addition to reporting on the extent of Russia's environmental calamity, Feshbach charts a strategy for Western institutions to follow to help "stop the bleeding." Foremost among his recommendations is the creation of a central institution responsible for coordinating the environmental and humanitarian aid provided by Western donor countries, international financial institutions, and nongovernmental organizations. Feshbach cites the example of the Intergovernmental Group for Indonesia, which coordinated aid to that region in the late 1960s, as a model. Even without additional funding from the U.S. government, some effort to improve the coordination of the myriad assistance efforts under way is sensible.

The overview Feshbach presents in the pages that follow is disturbing, even depressing. Simply dealing with the most pressing threats to public health seems beyond the current resources of the Soviet successor states. Regrettably, too, the West's contribution, if one discounts for present political realities, appears likely to fall very short of the mark.

Yet if we have learned anything at all from recent history, it is that we need to be cautious about labeling anything impossible. It may well be that the continuing evolution of public attitudes in the former Soviet Union and here in the West will make possible the serious efforts required to reverse environmental decline at some time in the near future. In fact, it is worth remembering how far we have come in the last few years: the problems are at last increasingly out in the open—thanks to Murray Feshbach and a handful of other investigators. On behalf of the Trustees of the Twentieth Century Fund, I thank him for his efforts.

This essay is the first of a series on "Russia in Transition" being sponsored by the Fund. In the next several months, we shall publish papers on the Russian health-care crisis by David E. Powell of Wheaton College, on defense conversion by MIT's Kevin O'Prey, and on labor by Linda J. Cook of Brown University.

Richard C. Leone, *President*
The Twentieth Century Fund
January 1995

CONTENTS

PREFACE

The purpose of this study is to go beyond description and analysis of the current environmental and health crises in the former Soviet Union by highlighting the principal issues that must be addressed and confronted by the Russian, American, and other governments, either alone or in concert through international agencies such as the World Bank, the European Bank for Reconstruction and Development, the European Union, and remarkable nongovernmental organizations such as ISAR (formerly the Institute for Soviet-American Relations), the American International Health Alliance, the Baltic Sea Commission, Ecologia, and others.

Clearly, this paper cannot examine all the environmental and health problems of the region and their potential impact on the world community; only those of the highest priority have been considered. Other analysts might consider different problems to be of higher priority than those selected for discussion here. To these analysts, I apologize for not addressing their concerns; it must be said that the issues emphasized here are more than sufficient to engage the communities involved in the crucial tasks at hand.

When I shared my initial draft of this study containing the analysis of these new environmental and health data with Dr. Sergei Bobylev, a professor at Moscow State University specializing in environmental economics, he commented that this new material could be even more useful to the policymaker than *Ecocide*. Primarily, Dr. Bobylev noted that in contrast to *Ecocide*, where we were forced to rely heavily on secondary reports, newspaper accounts, and conjecture, there are numerous scientific studies and empirical evidence released from Russian ministries and departments to back up the conclusions.

I owe a major debt to David Kenney, a former foreign service officer of the U.S. Department of State, now with the Center for Post-Soviet Studies, for his outstanding editorial efforts and for his contributions to developing the policy recommendations in this study. His experience with the Inter-governmental Group for Indonesia and suggestions for this model's analogous application to the former Soviet Union contributed significantly to the final version of this study.

Several other colleagues also provided invaluable assistance. I am particularly grateful to Dr. Gregory Guroff, director of Russian and Eurasian Studies at the Center for Post-Soviet Studies. Dr. Guroff made the original contact with the Twentieth Century Fund for the initiation of this study and also contributed his political insights, editorial comments, criticism, and encouragement. I must also thank Joshua Handler of Greenpeace, who kindly made available a number of his writings and documents that were very useful; Mr. Keith Bush, formerly of Radio Free Europe/Radio Liberty, now with the Center for Strategic and International Studies, for a vast array of materials from the RFE/RL information collection system; and Dr. Stanley Kober for providing me with many helpful items from the European press. I also wish to thank my research assistants (in alphabetical order)—Douglas A. R. Goudie, Janel R. Lardizabal, and Catherine M. Schaidler of Georgetown University—for their help in the preparation of this study.

Finally, I wish to thank the Twentieth Century Fund for its patience. I hope this book will meet its expectations and needs.

Murray Feshbach

ECOLOGICAL DISASTER

INTRODUCTION

The ecological catastrophe is not a threat to our country alone. . . . Without any fear of exaggeration, we can say that the survival of the human race will depend on its ability to solve this problem.[1]

In 1992 Alfred Friendly, Jr., and I published *Ecocide in the USSR*, a book that described the ecological damage inflicted on the Soviet Union. We concluded that "no other industrial civilization so systematically and so long poisoned its land, air, and people."[2] Russia suffered the brunt of the ecological destruction. Indeed, today some of the most threatening global environmental problems are found there. However, it is important to stress that the collapse of the Soviet Union left behind a legacy of ecological destruction and declining health conditions in all the territories of the former Soviet Union (hereafter FSU).

Since we wrote *Ecocide*, a great deal of enlightening information has become available detailing the extent and severity of the problem now facing the nations of the FSU. One of the more encouraging trends since the publication of *Ecocide* has been the increasing willingness of the Russian government to publish previously classified information about military and industrial programs that threaten the environment. In 1994 the Russian government enacted Article 7 of the State Secrets Act, requiring all federal agencies to publish environmental and health data without limits. From the first open publication of environmental statistics in 1988 to the present, an expansion of the number and type of data series, as well as their quality, has been noted. Dr. Alexey Yablokov's April 1993 report on radioactive waste and dumping at sea, while still far from complete or fully credible, serves as a principal example of this unprecedented disclosure of details about formerly secret operations.[3]

Early in 1993, Vladimir P. Vorfolomeyev, then head of the Russian Supreme Soviet's Committee on Ecological Questions and Rational Utilization of Natural Resources, released critical data not previously published, including information on the military sector's contribution to pollution.[4] These new data are supplemented by the numerous studies of health and ecological problems currently being undertaken by Dr. Yablokov in his position as head of the Interagency Ecological Security Committee of the Russian Federation's Security Council. The new openness about the publication of information by both government and private sources has significantly advanced Western understanding of the ecological and health crises facing the FSU.

The nuclear accident on April 6, 1993, at Tomsk-7, one of the secret cities in the Soviet nuclear network, prompted an order by President Boris Yeltsin to the State Committee for Nuclear and Radiation Safety Oversight (Gosatomnadzor) to undertake an inventory of all nuclear installations and other facilities that could pose a threat of radiation within the Russian Federation. Such facilities fall under the jurisdiction of numerous federal agencies, including the Ministry of Atomic Industry, the State Committee for the Defense Industry, the Ministry of Defense, the Ministry of Transportation and the Kurchatov Research Institute. In March 1993 it had been reported that within Moscow alone, fifty nuclear reactors had been deemed "unsafe"; two reactors at the Kurchatov Research Institute had been shut down.[5] However, some of the most dangerous facilities continued to operate. By the end of 1993 more than two hundred enterprises were examined, and Gosatomnadzor concluded that "Russia's nuclear power plants are incapable of maintaining their equipment in a safe state."[6]

Investigations of Russia's nuclear facilities have greatly increased outsiders' knowledge about formerly secret cities and nuclear operations within the Russian military-industrial complex. However, to date the military and the Ministry of Atomic Industry have continued to resist full inspection of their facilities by Gosatomnadzor and public disclosure of much information relating to nuclear safety. As late as June 1994 the Ministry of Defense had not yet approved the order by Yeltsin authorizing Gosatomnadzor's access. Ministerial veto rights apparently exceed those of the president. A *Segodnya* correspondent noted that "in practice, there is no federal supervision over the Defense Ministry's nuclear facilities."[7] The implication in the foregoing that Gosatomnadzor has no competence in the military realm of nuclear activities is not correct, or at least not completely correct.

The 1993 annual report of the Russian nuclear regulatory agency, available to the author only in the fall of 1994, provides a much clearer picture of the situation. The agency does have jurisdiction over some of the activities thought to be unregulated, but it does not have jurisdiction over all of the pertinent functions that nominally are under its scope and coverage. For example, the report lists numerous nuclear research reactor installations under Gosatomnadzor's observation, as well as enterprises producing equipment for these reactors, but the agency explicitly does not have jurisdiction over atomic weapons and nuclear-powered submarines belonging to the Ministry of Atomic Industry and the Ministry of Defense. The State Committee for the Defense Industry (Goskomoboronprom) has agreed to allow Gosatomnadzor full access: the Ministry of Atomic Industry's research and other activities at ten reactor sites, twelve industrial enterprises involved in the nuclear fuel cycle production process, nine ships of the Murmansk Shipping Company and twenty-six enterprises of the Goskomoboronprom's Shipbuilding Industry are explicitly named as subject to Gosatomnadzor's jurisdiction. Nonetheless, the Ministry of Defense and the Ministry of Atomic Industry are directly cited as "blocking the timely fulfillment of the Russian Presidential Order [of 16 September 1993]" granting Gosatomnadzor jurisdiction over all of their facilities to ensure nuclear safety. The two objecting ministries reported to the president's office in December 1993 that Gosatomnadzor should not have the right to inspect "nuclear hazardous sites and nuclear weapons and missiles, at various stages of development, construction, warehousing, transporting, and destruction."Thus, despite an explicit order signed by President Yeltsin, Gosatomnadzor has only a partial victory. Prospects for nuclear safety control overall remain negative if the lengthy list of problems at the ministries' sites already open to them are indicative of the problems at the still-closed facilities. Experience in dealing with the military, prior to President Yeltsin's order for a national nuclear inventory, supports Yablokov's judgment that "in what concerns chemical and biological conversion, the military does not tell us the whole truth and sometimes deceives us."[8] Many details about the clandestine network of cities with nuclear, chemical, and biological warfare facilities remain highly guarded.[9]

There have also been improvements in the publication of ecological and health data; however, questions of accuracy persist. Currently, the governments of the newly independent states are endeavoring to obtain more accurate health statistics. These efforts are being supported with the technical and financial assistance of the U.S. Public Health Service Centers for Disease Control and Prevention. Today the main obstacle is not ideological pressure from governmental authorities to withhold health data. Rather, the principal difficulty is internal disarray—particularly along the southern tier of the FSU (Transcaucasus and parts of Central Asia)—nonsubmission of data by local authorities, and reduced emphasis on the quality of statistical reporting. In addition, there is institutional resistance by many organizations and enterprises to compliance with health and environmental reporting requirements—particularly involving the disposal of toxic waste—because of fear that disclosure could lead to regulatory responses that would inhibit production or affect profitability.

Despite better reporting, insufficient attention is still being paid by the governments of Russia and other FSU countries to issues of environment and health. Environmental and health data tend to be fragmented, incomplete, and generally unreliable. Policy planners simply do not have adequate information upon to which to base a comprehensive attack on the major environment-induced health problems. This information gap exists not only for such areas as radioactive and chemical pollution of air, water, and land but also for industrial toxic wastes, heavy metals, and other causes of poor health.

One of the first tasks of the Western planner—if a serious attack on environmental and health problems is contemplated—will be to close this information gap. A number of Western countries, the World Bank, and the U.S. Agency for International Development (AID) have recognized the serious deficiency of health and environmental knowledge and are developing important programs to combat this problem. Dr. Elena Gurvich and Dr. Boris Revich, independent researchers working with AID, are doing commendable work in this area.

The research conducted by Gurvich and Revich, however, appears to be no longer a priority for support by AID because Western countries unfortunately have not designated the collection of environmental and health data as a task of great importance.[10] Improving the collection of environmental and health data is, however, a major emphasis of this paper and should be an overall goal of Western policies. This study will ultimately present recommendations regarding how such information could be better shared between donor countries and agencies and how indigenous health and environmental organizations could be better utilized in developing a policy consensus on these topics.

Closing the information gap will not be easy. During the last year, as I accumulated data for an environmental and health atlas, my Russian colleagues were reluctant to provide data on toxic waste, including heavy metals, due to the poor quality of such data. Preliminary data on industrial hazardous waste—from one unofficial and two official national inventories—were published only in 1990. The *State Report on the State of the Environment of the Russian Federation in 1992* devotes only limited space to the issues of nuclear, industrial, medical, household, and other wastes. The authors of the *State Report* appeared either to not understand the importance of the issue or to have inadequate data. They may also have been reluctant to focus too much attention on toxic waste emanating from the military-industrial complex.

At issue is not only the scope and coverage but also the quality of environmental and health information. Many experts concluded that available statistics on air pollution, for example, are 30 to 50 percent lower than the real figures. What data there are on air and water pollution are skewed by the lack of reporting from military-industrial complexes, military facilities, the nuclear weapons industry, and many agricultural production units. Communism may be dead, but Lenin's dictum that "statistics are not scholarly but practical" lives on. The normal bureaucratic response to requests for information is often to conceal what might be embarrassing or costly.

The inadequacy of existing environmental and health information undoubtedly adds to the uncertain and limited approach of the governments of Russia and other FSU countries in dealing with their pollution crisis. Russia's first environmental legislation, the Law on Environmental Protection signed by President Yeltsin in December 1991, is a compendium of policy declarations covering every conceivable environmental issue, but it provides no adequate legal framework for regulatory or corrective action. The draft federal law "On State Policy in the Field of Handling Radioactive Wastes" calls for a five-year (1994–99), 34 million-ruble program to draft future regulations and statutes, with no funding for actual cleanup activities.

The information that is available, particularly in terms of health data, is worrisome. Indications are that, with rare exception, basic

standards have deteriorated throughout the FSU since the 1992 publication of *Ecocide in the USSR*. Mortality has increased dramatically,
morbidity in some categories is nearing epidemic levels, and life
expectancy—now at a thirty-year low—continues to decline (see
Figure 1). In the first six months of 1993 deaths exceeded births by 100
percent throughout all of Russia, and by 160 percent in Moscow and St.
Petersburg; in all of 1993, deaths exceeded births by about 750,000
persons. Existing data—which appear to seriously underestimate the
problem because of various statistical errors of commission, omis-
sion, and general noncompliance with international WHO methodology—show that infant mortality has increased dramatically over the
last year, up to 19.9 deaths per 1,000 live births (from 17 in 1992; see
Figure 2); it may be as high as 30 per 1,000 when underestimation is
incorporated in an adjusted estimate. (In contrast, the U.S. figure of 8.6

FIGURE 1
LIFE EXPECTANCY AT BIRTH IN RUSSIA
1980–1993

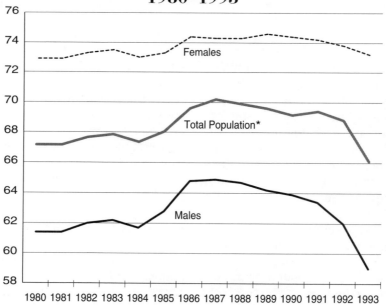

* Estimates for 1980–86, 1990, and 1993 based on average of reported male and
female figures.

Source: Goskomstat RSFSR, *Demograficheskiye perspektivy Rossii*, 1993, p. 21.

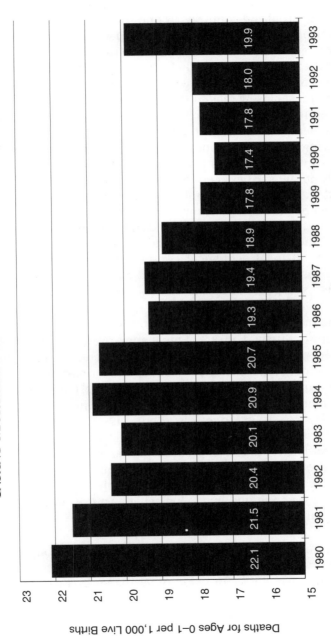

FIGURE 2
INFANT MORTALITY RATE IN RUSSIA 1980–1993

Deaths for Ages 0–1 per 1,000 Live Births

Sources: Tsentr demografii i ekologii cheloveka, *Naseleniye Rossii; yezhegodnyy demograficheskiy doklad,* 1993, p. 50; interview with Colonel General E. A. Nechayev, RSFSR Minister of Health, by *Argumenty i Fakty,* as reported in Foreign Broadcast Information System, FBIS-USR-93-157, December 15, 1993, pp. 41–42.

infant deaths per 1,000 live births in 1993, far from the best record among industrialized countries, is one-third of the adjusted Russian figure.) Neonatal death (death during the first week of life) was studied over nine years in seven cities and in seven rural *rayons* in Chelyabinsk oblast (where the secret city Chelyabinsk-65 is located) inhabited by about two million people all told. The rate of infant mortality turned out to be most closely related to the levels of nitrogen dioxide emissions and hydrocarbons. These pollutants appear correlated with about 60 percent of the infant mortality.[11]

During this same period, there was a major decrease—by one million—in the number of births reported in Russia (see Figure 3). Probably no statistic better epitomizes the current societal crisis facing Russia than that there are two abortions for every three pregnancies.[12]

Other health statistics show that, in 1992, 75 percent of all women in Russia suffered from a pathology during pregnancy. Reproductive health is one of the most accurate indicators of public health overall, as well as of local ecological conditions, the Interdepartmental Commission of the Security Council on Ecological Safety concluded in 1994. In this respect, Russia has cause for concern:

> The rate of severe pregnancy complications is constantly rising in Russia. The rate of pregnancy-related toxemia rose by 41 percent between 1981 and 1989, representing 7.7 per 100 births. Furthermore, cases of severe forms of toxemia— eclampsia and preeclampsia—increased 4.8 fold. Pregnant women were 2.6 times as likely to suffer from anemia, twice as likely to suffer kidney disorders, and 21.9 percent more likely to suffer from cardiovascular disease.
>
> Although the rate of prenatal problems has risen everywhere, the rise is more pronounced in large industrial centers, where many women are employed in jobs with hazardous working conditions [and living in highly unsatisfactory ecological conditions].[13]

Maternal death in childbirth—which is now probably 20 to 30 percent undercounted due to flaws in Soviet/Russian statistical methodology—is still six or seven times higher in Russia than in the United States. Only 40 percent of all children can be considered "healthy" at birth.[14] The illness rate among newborns more than doubled, from 82.4 per 1000 live births in 1980 to 173.7 in 1991. In St.

FIGURE 3
CRUDE BIRTH AND DEATH RATES IN RUSSIA 1980–1993

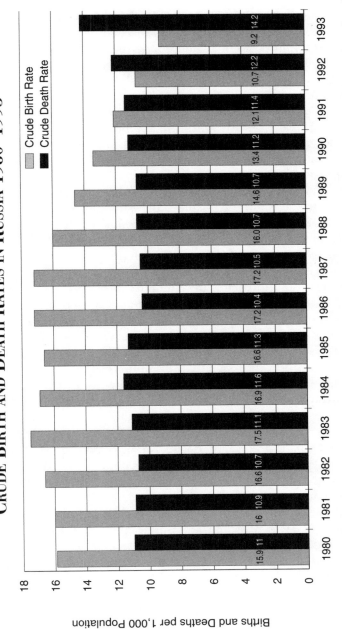

Sources: Goskomstat SSSR, *Demograficheskiy yezgegodnik SSSR*, 1990, p. 99; Goskomstat RSFSR, *Zdravookhraneniye v Rossiiskoy Federatsii*, 1992, p. 3; interview with Colonel General E. A. Nechayev, RSFSR Minister of Health, by *Argumenty i Fakty*, as reported in Foreign Broadcast Information Service, FBIS-USR-93-158, December 15, 1993, pp. 41–42.

Petersburg, a tiny fraction (3 to 4 percent) of all children were considered "healthy" several years ago, according to the chief pediatrician of the city; now only .7 percent are considered healthy.[15]

According to Dr. Galina Serdyukovskaya from the Ministry of Health, 40 to 45 percent of all children in the USSR in 1991 exhibited functional disorders that could, in adverse conditions, lead to serious illness. Between 25 to 35 percent of Russia's children suffered from chronic illnesses.[16] Subsequent data affirm this pattern, suggesting that conditions are even worse.

"The situation is truly catastrophic," is how the director of an institute dealing with maternal and child health summed up the juvenile health situation in Russia.[17] In most cases, medical care, immunizations, and medicines are less available today (if at all) than several years ago due to lack of medicines, disrepair of facilities, emigration of physicians, and the rejection by hospitals of terminally ill patients. "More than 200,000 of our children die every year due to our inability to give them prompt and high-quality medical care," *Pravda* reported in 1990. "Every year 5,000 children are in need of bone marrow transplants alone. Such operations generally are not performed on children here."[18] Overall, the proportion of healthy children is probably less than 20 percent in Russia. Moreover, national statistics show a rising number of birth defects such as cleft palates, cerebral palsy, and spina bifida. Government figures show that the number of babies with obvious deformities rose 6 percent nationwide in the first eight months of 1993 compared with 1992.[19] In one republic of Russia, Bashkortostan, congenital anomalies are ten times higher than in the United States.[20]

The Deputy Minister of Public Health, Nikolay Vaganov, was quite correct to conclude that "Russia stands on the edge of an abyss." He continued, "For the first time in its centuries-old history, there is a danger of the nation's physical degeneration, of irreparable damage to its genetic fund."[21] This characterization echoes the words of academician V. Pokrovskiy, head of the Russian Academy of Medical Sciences, who noted at the time of the publication of the first Russian *State Report on the State of Health of the Population of the Russian Federation in 1992*, Moscow, 1993, that "we [Russia] have already doomed ourselves for the next 25 years."[22]

Unsheltered and crowded conditions among forced migrants, refugees, and illegal immigrants have added to the decline in health standards and have probably contributed to the decline in population growth in the FSU. Unfortunately, the total impact of inadequate housing and sanitation for migrants is not yet known because refugee morbidity often goes unreported or is underreported owing to the absence of health-care facilities to serve them. One report, incomplete as it may be, estimates that 40 percent of Kurdish refugee children in the Moscow area have tuberculosis.

Refugees often do not have access to medicine or medical equipment. Russia produces only 15–28 percent of medicines it requires;[23] in Kazakhstan probably less than 5 percent of all medicine is produced domestically. Throughout the FSU, the medicine that is available to the local population is expensive because it has to be imported and is often sold for hard currency. In fact, availability of affordable medicine and vitamins has become one of the most difficult problems confronting the health sector. There is also a serious deficiency in basic diagnostic equipment throughout the FSU. For example, in three polyclinics in Moscow where approximately eighteen thousand patients suffer from ischemic heart conditions, fewer than 1,500 cholesterol tests are administered per year. That is to say, the overwhelming majority of these heart patients do not have this vital test even once a year.[24] Within Russia in recent years, there has been an astonishing increase in infectious diseases, reflecting a breakdown in both sanitation and immunization services (see Figure 4, p. 14). Soviet immunization programs were always erratic at best, more effective in urban than rural areas, treating more registered inhabitants rather than illegal migrants, while failing to contend with certain diseases (such as rubella) at all. However, since 1992 the situation has become noticeably worse. Garbage has piled up in the streets of Moscow and other cities. Large refugee and migrant camps now have attached themselves to most major urban areas. Disposable syringes and needles became, for a period, generally unavailable. More of the population was becoming sick, and yet fewer medical workers were offering immunizations or other services. Children who had various illnesses were often determined not to be eligible for vaccinations. Fear of AIDS transmitted by unclean syringes and needles prevented many others seeking immunizations for themselves or their families. Statistics show that at present only slightly more than 50 percent of the children in Russia are fully inoculated.[25]

The complete slide in the quality of health in the FSU is probably best demonstrated by the dramatic increase in diphtheria cases in Russia (see Figure 5, p. 15). In the last three years the number of cases has increased by a factor of thirteen, from 1,200 in 1990 to 15,210 in 1993.[26] In the first three months of 1994 alone, diphtheria has been recorded at about quadruple the rate of the previous year, or 6,136 for the first three months. If this trend continues there may be 35,000 to 40,000 cases of diphtheria in 1994. Even before this latest surge in new cases, the Finnish government had issued a warning to its citizens about their next-door neighbor. The government of Finland is also concerned about the renewed spread of polio and rabies from Russia to Finland.[27] These concerns may lead Finland to exercise greater control in preventing Russians from entering the country without proof of immunization.

Although less dramatic, there has also been a significant increase in other infectious and parasitic diseases such as typhoid, hepatitis, helminths, tuberculosis (a 22 percent increase in the first three months of 1994 over the same period the previous year), measles (a 260 percent

FIGURE 4
CHILD IMMUNIZATION RATES IN RUSSIA 1989–1992

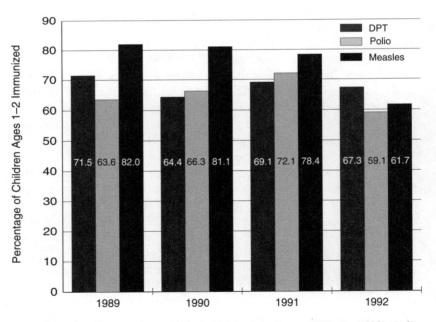

Source: UNICEF International Child Development Center (ICDC), *Public Policy and Social Conditions,* Regional Monitoring Report, Central and Eastern Europe in Transition, Number 1 (November 1993): 84.

increase), and mumps (a 10 percent increase). In addition, there has now been a significant increase in the incidence of cholera in Dagestan, Chechnya, and Moscow.

Considering the current situation, the focus of any Western program should be on women and children, particularly pre- and postnatal care. The plight of older generations may seem equally compelling: after all, there has also been a dramatic increase (by 30 percent) over the last year in deaths among males at prime working age (16 to 59). However, there may not be the time or the money to save that older, "Soviet" generation if maternity and children's health is given first priority, as should be. Comparisons of cause-of-death data by the

FIGURE 5
REGISTERED CASES OF DIPHTHERIA IN RUSSIA
1985–1993
(Per 100,000 Population)

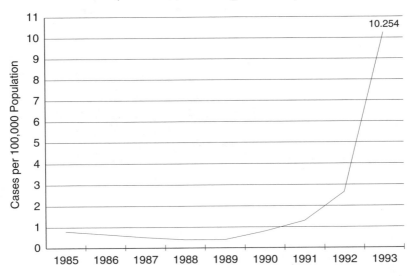

Sources: Goskomsanepidnadzor Rossii, *Zdorov'ye naseleniya i sreda obitaniya,* No. 1, 1994, p. 22. Goskomstat Rossii, *Zdravookhraneniye v Rossiyskoy Federatsii,* Moscow, 1992, p. 20. Goskomstat Rossii, *Narodnoye khozyaystvo Rossiyskoy Federatsii 1992,* Moscow, 1992, p. 279. Goskomstat Rossii, *Okhrana zdorov'ya v RSFSR v 1990 g.,* Moscow, 1991, pp. 77–105. Ministerstvo zdravookhraneniya SSSR, *Zdravookhraneniye v SSSR,* Moscow, 1989, pp. 9–10.

FIGURE 6

CAUSES OF DEATH, USSR AND DEVELOPED CAPITALIST COUNTRIES (U.S., GERMANY, FRANCE, GREAT BRITAIN, JAPAN) POPULATION IN ABLE-BODIED AGES,* BY SEX: 1987

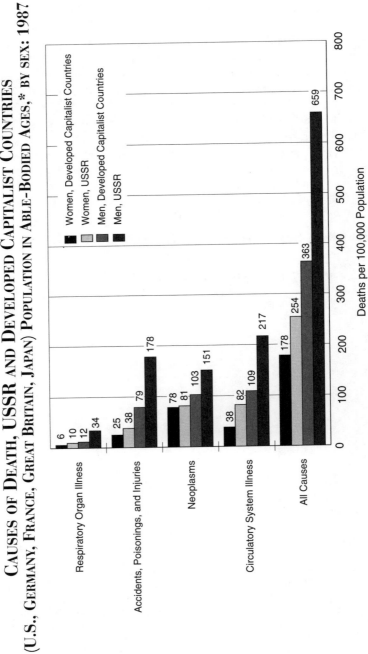

* Able-bodied ages defined as 16–59 years for men and 16–54 years for women, inclusive.
Source: Goskomstat SSSR, *Press-vypusk,* Number 191, May, 1989, p. 2.

State Statistical Agency demonstrates how far behind the health of the population is in comparison with the West (see Figure 6).

Based on the information available, it is now clear that the breadth and depth of the health and environmental problems of the FSU have been understated. In addition, previous studies failed to stress the threat the latter now pose to global ecology. Most Western experts today agree that the breakup of the Soviet Union and the Warsaw Pact has exposed what one reporter called "a dire environmental legacy": Strewn throughout the FSU are polluted, abandoned military sites, industrial plants dating from the 1940s and 1950s, unsafe nuclear power plants, and water-diversion projects that have caused large-scale desertification and erosion.[28]

The general societal crisis in the former Eastern bloc has been developing for decades through accumulated policy mistakes, environmental blindness, and simple contempt for the average citizen. All key social indices—declining living standards, hyperinflation, rising crime, growing alcoholism, increased abortion rates—now point to a social fabric that is under extreme pressure and is beginning to come apart. A UNICEF analysis of the crisis in Central and Eastern Europe concluded that:

> If the evidence presented in this report is correct, some of these countries—Albania and Russia in particular—are experiencing a process of social disintegration which has reached truly alarming proportions. This evidence, in particular, is indicative of a far deeper malaise than could have been expected, even from the transformation of an ailing economy and authoritarian state.[29]

The environmental and health data only fill in the grim outline of a population facing a desperate future. The monetary and physical cost of reversing the course of and preventing future environmental destruction has not yet been determined. It took decades to create the current ecological and health crisis; no doubt it will take decades to repair the damage. Yablokov points to three problems that urgently need resolution because of the clear threat they pose to global environment: First, Russia must avoid another "Chernobyl catastrophe." Second, it must eliminate the threat to the Arctic Ocean and the Baltic and Japan Seas from nuclear and other toxic waste dumping. Third, it must stop the wanton destruction of its forests.[30]

It is important for the West to recognize the serious societal, economic, environmental, and health crisis currently unfolding in the FSU. For the West to ignore this problem would be an act of considerable indifference and callousness in the face of a clear humanitarian crisis. Not to mention it could also be a significant political mistake, risking the hostility of future generations toward Europe and the United States. Not everything can be done at once. However, the West needs to act quickly to provide the most basic humanitarian assistance to the afflicted populations. A strategy must be set up to tackle the problems that will take decades to solve.

Chapter 1

A Nuclear Plague

The FSU is today awash with nuclear materials. There is no better way to characterize the recent disclosures of toxic, radioactive dumping and unsafe nuclear practices by the Russian and other successor governments. In the last two years, many unofficial nuclear dump sites have been found, and more data on radioactive pollution have been accumulated. This information has raised a number of critical questions about the operational safety of nuclear industries and research centers. Most of these nuclear facilities are part of a network of "secret cities" that have only recently been revealed to the West.

These revelations have opened a number of new lines of investigation. Among the more important studies currently under way are:

- evaluations of the true extent of radioactive contamination emanating from the Chernobyl accident (see Chapter 2);

- evaluations of the impact on health of the Chernobyl disaster;

- investigations of nuclear waste dumping, particularly in the waters of the Arctic and Pacific oceans;

- analyses of the number, location, and condition of nuclear-powered submarines awaiting dismantling;

- analyses of the handling and disposal of radioactive materials by research institutes, the pharmaceutical industry, hospitals, and health facilities;

- investigations of the "secret city" network of the nuclear and chemical sectors of the military-industrial complex;

- analyses of the lack of security at nuclear facilities sparked by concerns about theft of nuclear materials, smuggling, and potential use by terrorist organizations or unfriendly governments;

- evaluations of unsafe operation of facilities using radioactive materials that could lead to accidents such as occurred in April 1993 at Tomsk-7, in July 1993 at Chelyabinsk-65, and in June 1994 at Kamchatka;

- evaluations of poor safety procedures and ongoing infractions of rules and regulations for the operation of RBMK and other types of civilian nuclear reactors that could lead to an escape of radioactive nuclides similar to what occurred at Chernobyl, as well as lack of proper containment structures; and

- analysis of data suggesting that no amount of retrofitting or equipment upgrade is likely to make the oldest types of nuclear generators safe.

THE SPREAD OF RADIOACTIVE WASTE

As of early 1993 radioactive materials were reportedly produced, used, and stored in 320 cities and 1,548 other locations within Russia. One source cited more than 260 areas of radioactive contamination throughout the Russian Federation, 40 of which had radioactivity levels greater than one milliroentgen per hour.[1] In the fall of 1993 a Russian journalist compared the spread of radioactive waste to a "Nuclear Plague."[2] To illustrate the point, he referred to a map of radioactive contamination of Russia showing 140 *rayons* (equivalent to a county within the United States) and 7,700 populated communities seriously affected by radioactive pollution. At the Kurchatov Center and other research installations in Moscow, there is reportedly in excess of 200 tons of radioactive waste.[3]

In June 1994 four State Duma (parliament) committees held hearings on the handling of radioactive waste at some 14,500 enterprises where there were more than 700 sources of radiation all told.[4] Based on the data released by Vorfolomeyev, these included industrial enterprises, research institutions, military organizations, and nuclear power plants.[5] According to Gosatomnadzor the least safe handling of radioactive waste was at enterprises attached to the Ministry of Defense and the Ministry of Atomic Industry.[6]

New discoveries of industrial and commercial radioactive waste— from above-ground explosions, uranium ore processing, the chemical industry, metallurgical plants, power plants, and medical facilities (the pharmaceutical industry, hospitals, and research institutes)—are regularly being made. Much more is also being revealed about past dumping practices. For example, in January 1994 an official of the Ministry of Atomic Energy, attempting to refute claims that one ton of plutonium was buried in a lake in the Tomsk region about twenty years ago, admitted that all the radioactive waste from the Siberian Chemical Plant in Tomsk, with a radioactivity of one billion curies, had been buried underground in an area with subsoil waters, potentially allowing radioactivity to spread further.[7]

This excess of radioactive waste has come about largely because the former Soviet states use much more radioactive material than any other countries. "Every month we learn something new about this," Yablokov commented in 1993. He added that in Moscow alone the authorities find about fifty new radioactively contaminated sites annually.[8] At the July 1993 joint meeting of International Atomic Energy Agency (IAEA) and United Nations Development Programme (UNDP) in Vienna, various ministers of environment of the ex-Soviet countries or their representatives reported that in Ukraine 100,000 small nuclear power plants exist; in Moldova, 11,000. In Latvia, even without a local nuclear industry, more than seven hundred cubic meters of radioactive waste from medical and pharmaceutical industries has been buried. These and other revelations were cited by Reinhart Helmke, head of the Division for Europe and the Commonwealth of Independent States (CIS) of the UNDP, at a speech in Copenhagen to launch a joint effort with the IAEA to improve the nuclear safety infrastructure in the FSU.[9]

Beyond the revelations at the IAEA/UNDP conference, Kazakh geologists have found about eight million tons of radioactive waste in their country. Officials can cite 529 radioactive waste and burial sites. Much of this contamination is the result of seventeen nuclear tests carried out on one test range in the Atyrau oblast since the mid-1960s. Kazakh authorities are now trying to bury the contaminated soil at this site. However, in the areas where the tests took place, nuclear sites are practically unfenced. There is no transportation decontamination station, and reportedly the soil is picked up by vehicles and spread throughout the district.[10]

Belarus also has large quantities of radioactive materials at the so-called Facility 802 near Brest. Spent uranium from East European nuclear plants was routinely transferred through this site to the reprocessing facilities at Krasnoyarsk-26 in Siberia.[11] But during the transition from a single Soviet state to independent governments, Belarus has not been able to transfer the materials to Russia because no intergovernmental agreement exists.

For a period of time, Ukraine also found that it could not ship radioactive waste from its nuclear power plants to Russia. Moscow blocked these shipments principally in order to put pressure on Kiev over the issue of control of nuclear weapons located in Ukraine. Currently it is possible for Ukraine to ship nuclear waste, but only for short periods of time because all nuclear waste storage facilities in Russia are either full, close to being full, inadequate, or, for political reasons, the Russian government can put pressure on Ukraine to "cooperate" with them.

Among the more controversial recent proposals for the elimination of nuclear and chemical waste has been one that would use underground nuclear explosions. The Novaya Zemlya test site was recommended for this purpose in 1994 by Major-General Vladimir Loborev, head of the Central Physics and Technical Institute of the Ministry of Defense, and Alexander Chernyshov, deputy head of the All-Russia Research and Development Institute of Experimental Physics at Arzamas-16.[12] These scientists argue that the conventional method of dealing with high level nuclear waste—vitrification—is too expensive, requiring twenty plants working for ten years to dispose of Russia's nuclear waste. Their proposal involves putting large quantities of radioactive waste in a deep shaft and then exploding a nuclear device to bury the waste permanently.

HIGHLY ENRICHED URANIUM AND PLUTONIUM

New data have forced a radical revision upward of prior estimates of the quantities of the highly enriched uranium (HEU) and weapons-grade plutonium currently stored in Russia. In fact, the supplies of uranium and plutonium are higher than ever because of wide-scale dismantling of nuclear weapons. In February 1993 the United States signed an agreement to purchase from Russia 500 tons of HEU for $12 billion, assuming that this represented most of Russia's supply.[13] Since then, the minister of atomic industry, Viktor Mikhaylov, has indicated that there are more than 1,200 tons of stockpiled highly enriched uranium.[14] Based on the previous selling price, if the United States plans to purchase these additional 700 tons, $16.8 billion more will need to be appropriated. In May 1994 the Clinton administration officially asked Moscow to disclose just how much highly enriched uranium and plutonium Russia holds and where it can be found.[15]

Meanwhile, the Russian government continues to produce new HEU. An article in *Trud* noted that in order to provide nuclear fuel for a single reactor in a nuclear submarine, about 75 tons of uranium ore must be enriched, 99.8 percent of which eventually becomes waste.[16] Similarly, approximately 500,000 tons of uranium ore must be processed to fill an RBMK-1000 reactor (such as the one at Chernobyl). Again, 99.8 percent becomes waste.[17]

With regard to plutonium, ITAR-TASS reports that storage sites in Russia are now filled to the limit with weapons-grade material and plutonium released from dismantled nuclear weapons. General William Burns, head of the U.S. government delegation to Russia, testified in the spring of 1993 that there were estimated to be 50 tons of plutonium in storage in Russia.[18] New information suggests that there are actually 100 to 150 tons.[19] The Russian government continues to process new plutonium.[20]

In March 1994 U.S. Department of Energy secretary Hazel O'Leary and atomic industry minister Mikhaylov concluded a deal under which Russia will shut down three nuclear reactors producing weapons-grade plutonium as soon as alternative sources for the heating of local communities can be made available.[21] In order to achieve this the United States agreed to help Russia find the money to pay for the new heating plants. The Russian government has announced that the three plants will be closed at the end of 1994.[22] However, Russian nuclear safety experts remain skeptical that this timetable can be met for "technical" reasons.[23] The last Krasnoyarsk reactor will not be closed until the turn of the century.

RENEWED FOCUS ON CHERNOBYL

New revelations regarding the Chernobyl accident have raised Russian consciousness about the potential danger of the older Soviet nuclear reactors. Parliamentarian and journalist Alla Yaroshinskaya has been active in analyzing the heretofore secret documents of the Working Group of the Politburo. In her book *Chernobyl': sovershenno sekretno* (*Chernobyl: Top Secret*), she examined the causes and effects of the Chernobyl catastrophe.[24] Yaroshinskaya reproduced 325 pages of secret documents from the archives of the Politburo of the Communist Party of the Soviet Union. In an April 1993 *Izvestiya* article, she analyzed a top secret, single-copy document to which she had just gained access,[25] and she provided the previously undisclosed complete text of a report on Chernobyl given before the Politburo of the CPSU Central Committee in July 1986.

Yaroshinskaya's revelations highlighted the investigating committee's admission of critical design flaws at Chernobyl. She claimed that its original report acknowledged design defects in the control and safety system rods of the reactor; however, such information was omitted from the report on the Chernobyl accident sent to the International Atomic Energy Agency (IAEA) in an attempt to conceal the truth. Yaroshinskaya also asserted that poor construction and unreliable instruments played an important role in the Chernobyl catastrophe. The Soviet government maintained instead that human error and violations of safety rules and operational procedures were to blame for the accident.[26]

There have been growing concerns about the sarcophagus and the remains of the burnt-out reactor at Chernobyl Unit Four. Based on information obtained by the French Institute for Nuclear Protection and Safety (INPS), inside the sarcophagus,

> slumbering deceptively, lie 64,000 cubic meters of radioactive materials, 800 to 1,000 tons of radioactive water, 35 tons of core fragments, 135 tons of "lava" produced by the partial fusing of core, concrete, and steel, and ten to fifteen tons of fuel in the form of fine dust that penetrates everywhere and encumbers the countryside with monitoring and sampling operations.[27]

There are about 11,000 square feet of cracks and openings in block number four's sarcophagus at Chernobyl.[28] Yuri Shcherbak, the former Ukrainian minister of environment, and other leading observers in Ukraine have warned that the release of additional radioactivity could leak into the Kiev aquifer or into the atmosphere.

Plans to construct a new sarcophagus around the old sarcophagus, which was built hastily after the 1986 accident, may court danger of additional contamination of the land and water. Environmentalists such as Svyatislav Zabelin, head of the Socio-Ecological Union, worry that the weight of a new concrete structure could lead to a shift in the subsurface land causing the roof to fall from its precarious support atop one of the walls in the now "contained" structure.[29] As a result there would be a release of additional quantities of radioactive dust into the atmosphere and unburned radioactive fuel into the rest of the building.

The sarcophagus was built to last twenty to thirty years, but some experts have warned that it may last at most seven years. While the more grim estimates have proven to be erroneous, the sarcophagus clearly will not last for another twenty-five years. According to an Institute for Nuclear Protection and Safety (INPS) official, "Repairs are difficult, since the radioactive exposure rate can reach as high as fifty rems per hour on the roof (the maximum legally permissible dose of ionizing radiation to which workers can be exposed is five rems per year) and between 300 and 1,000 rems per hour in the main hall."[30] There are also questions as to the ability of protective suits to adequately shield workers.[31]

THE POTENTIAL FOR NUCLEAR THEFT

Thousands of former Soviet nuclear technicians are experiencing declining living standards or are facing outright dismissal from their jobs. These technicians, some of whom are highly trained nuclear specialists, represent a talent pool that is highly vulnerable to lucrative offers by third world countries and terrorist organizations seeking to acquire a nuclear weapons capability. Beyond knowhow, the presence of nuclear material itself offers a temptation some might find hard to resist. In addition to the previously mentioned stocks of highly enriched uranium and weapons-grade plutonium, there are more than thirty thousand nuclear warheads located throughout the FSU, some nineteen thousand of which are currently waiting to be dismantled in Russia.[32]

The safeguarding of nuclear weapons, nuclear material, and nuclear "bomb-making" knowhow has increasingly become a concern for Western intelligence. Over the last several years it has been the subject of some of the highest-level U.S. government discussions with

Russia and other FSU states where nuclear weapons facilities are located. The Russian government itself has publicly taken the position that the worst scenario—the theft of a nuclear device—could not happen. Major-General Vitaly N. Yakovlev, deputy chief of the Russian Defense Ministry's nuclear directorate, told the Moscow newspaper *Literaturnaya gazeta* that "it is absolutely impossible to lose a warhead" because his agency maintains a database that records the location and contents of every nuclear warhead and personnel have access to warheads only in groups of three or more.[33] Perhaps, perhaps not.

Western experts, including officials in the U.S. Defense Department, have not been reassured by Russian confidence in their ability to maintain control over nuclear weaponry and especially material. "There are warheads and [nuclear] material scattered all over Russia, the inventories are not very good and there are turf fights between agencies over who gets to control it," according to Leonard S. Spector of the Carnegie Endowment for International Peace.[34]

According to journalist Seymour Hersh, the Natural Resource Defense Council proposed to the Bush administration in 1991 that the United States and Russia establish a joint program to find, identify, and tag all nuclear weapons in Russian and American stockpiles. The White House rejected the proposal because it was uncomfortable with the idea of reciprocal access to tactical and strategic nuclear storage areas.[35]

The Russian military, which has drawn the primary assignment of guarding nuclear depots, has itself been significantly weakened since the breakup of the Soviet empire. The military suffers from poor morale, lack of housing, increased drug use, and widespread hazing of recruits. Some elite units assigned to prevent terrorist attacks on nuclear weapons have been disbanded or have broken apart. Now their members are offering their "expertise" for sale.[36] One newspaper quotes an unnamed Russian military official as saying in 1993 that Russian military personnel had become the primary suppliers of black market weaponry on the territory of the FSU, particularly in the Caucasus region. The official claimed that 25,000 firearms had disappeared over the past six months, including 21,000 in the Caucasus.[37] By all reports, despite official Russian statements to the contrary, physical security at nuclear installations is vastly inferior to that at similar installations in the West. This condition undoubtedly reflects the old Soviet state's confidence that, backed up by a vast police and intelligence apparatus, it did not require sophisticated and expensive physical security systems.

If the Russian military cannot adequately carry out its charged duties because of budgetary and morale problems that undermine efforts to ensure the safety of nuclear weapons and material, other agencies of the Russian government currently are in no position to take over the job either. The table of organization for Gosatomnadzor lists a staff of 350 persons; in the spring of 1993 only 60 percent of that number were on the payroll.[38] Thus only a small proportion of the Gosatomnadzor staff members are available to examine plant and accident sites.

Despite a presidential directive to enhance nondepartmental supervision of nuclear enterprises,[39] the military still continues to refuse Gosatomnadzor access to some of its facilities and to limit access to others. General Yevgeniy Maslin, chief of the 12th Main Directorate, which deals with planning, censtruction, and operation of nuclear weapons facilities, is believed to be the source of much of the resistance to outside inspection.[40]

Disarray in the economy, an unstable social situation, ongoing political turmoil, nonpayment of wages to personnel, and recurring threats of "strikes" at various "secret" facilities, including Arzamas-16, Chelyabinsk-65, and the Baykonur Cosmodrome, have created the kind of conditions under which nuclear facilities could become vulnerable. "Nobody ever contemplated the Soviet military-industrial complex would end up in Chapter 11," commented Russell Seitz, an associate at Harvard's Center for Strategic Studies, in 1991. "It's the yard sale at the end of history."[41] Sergei P. Bogdanov, a spokesman for the Federal Counterintelligence Service (a successor to the KGB) has stated, "When the people in our country hear that for three kilograms of [radioactive] mercury you can get $1,000, no one thinks about the danger. They only think of how much they can earn."[42]

Fueling this concern about potential theft of nuclear material has been the clear interest of the Russian mafia in such illegal commerce. In May 1994 FBI Director Louis J. Freeh and First Deputy Minister of the Interior Mikhail Yegorov warned a Senate Government Affairs Committee that organized criminal groups were trying to infiltrate military facilities to steal nuclear materials to sell on the black market. "These crime groups in recent years are demonstrating more and more interest toward the defense facilities of the former Soviet Union," Yegorov told the Senate panel.[43] Freeh pointed to "a mounting threat to the safety and well-being" of Americans because of the possibility that such groups could obtain nuclear weapons materials or even a complete nuclear bomb.[44] A two-person FBI office has recently been established in Moscow to pursue these matters and other issues of mutual interest (narcotics in particular).

Until August of 1994, no *significant* amounts of HEU or pluto-nium—let alone a nuclear device—were known to have been stolen. However, Hersh reported that in 1991 Greenpeace came close to suc-cessfully negotiating a deal with a Russian lieutenant in Germany to steal a nuclear warhead for roughly $250,000. The proposed theft, undertaken to publicize how easy it was to obtain nuclear weapons, apparently only failed when the abortive Moscow coup in August resulted in the sudden transfer of nuclear weapons back to Russia.[45] By the end of August 1994, the German and Russian governments had apprehended a number of groups attempting to smuggle sub-stantial quantities of plutonium and uranium.

CIA director R. James Woolsey has testified about the estab-lishment of "smuggling networks that could be used to move such material. . . . " Much smuggling is carried on by, or at least with the knowledge of, industrial managers and governmental officials. "Formerly, there was a rigid system of export control," comment-ed acting Deputy Assistant Secretary of State Michael Newlin dur-ing a 1993 visit to the non-Russian states of the FSU to strengthen export controls. "In a period of a year and half, the system has disappeared."[46]

Given the collapse of the old police state, the rise in all forms of crime, and the porous nature of the borders of the onetime Soviet republics, no one has a definite idea how much nuclear material has in fact been stolen and taken out of the country. What is known is largely anecdotal:

- Ten kilograms of uranium were stolen by staff members of the secret facility at Arzamas-16 in December 1992.[47]

- Six lead blocks, each weighing 18 kg and containing cesium-137, a highly radioactive isotope, were stolen in 1992 from the Fosforit Association in Russia and smuggled into Estonia.[48]

- A lead capsule containing 5.5 lbs of uranium oxide was recov-ered in December 1992 in Brest (western Belarus) before it could be passed on to Polish accomplices. The uranium had been stolen from a secret facility 1,200 miles to the east.[49]

- The director general of the Estonian police in March 1993 accused two local Russian military commanders and several high-ranking officers of selling at least five highly radioactive metal products, including cesium-137, to Western dealers.[50]

- A container weighing 28 kg and containing cesium was recovered in July 1993 in Estonia from two Swedes who were trying to load it onto a ship heading for Sweden.[51]

- The Russian Federation Federal Counterintelligence Service in March 1994 arrested a group of people in St. Petersburg trying to sell more than three kilograms of highly enriched uranium dioxide to foreign buyers.[52]

- German authorities discovered in May 1994 in the garage of a Stuttgart businessman one-fifth of an ounce of weapons-grade plutonium-239, which apparently originated at a nuclear arms plant in Russia.[53] German authorities warned, though Russia denied this report, that up to 264 pounds of weapons-grade plutonium was being offered on the black markets of Europe.[54]

- Bavarian police seized .028 ounces of uranium-235 in June 1994 in Landshut. They arrested a Czech man, four Slovaks, and a forty-eight-year-old German woman, suspected to be the ringleader.[55]

- St. Petersburg officials prevented the theft of 6.6 pounds of weapons-grade uranium (presumably highly enriched) in the summer of 1994.[56]

- German officials seized the largest quantity yet of potential weapons-grade plutonium (plutonium-239) on August 10, 1994, at the Munich airport on a Lufthansa flight from Moscow. Originally officials indicated that they had seized between 100 and 500 grams; most recent estimates put the figure at 300 to 350 grams. They arrested two Spaniards and a Colombian in the incident.[57]

- Kaliningrad officials arrested three men attempting to sell a metal container of "unspecified, highly radioactive material" on August 15, 1994.[58]

- German authorities seized 0.05 grams of plutonium-239 from a thirty-four-year-old German man on August 16, 1994.[59]

- Moscow authorities apprehended two men on August 24, 1994, with 21 pounds of uranium-238, which they had taken from a secret nuclear center.[60]

First Deputy Minister of the Interior Mikhail Yegorov, who appeared with FBI director Louis J. Freeh before a Senate panel in May 1994, confirmed that over the preceding eighteen months his ministry investigated forty-seven criminal cases involving the theft of radioactive material, including nine alleged thefts of highly enriched materials required for nuclear weapons. Noting that only one such theft involved an organized crime group, Yegorov nevertheless argued that the danger must be taken more seriously.[61] Yegorov's comment was followed up a day later by a press statement in Moscow by Sergei Stepashin, chief of the Federal Counterintelligence Service, the domestic branch of the reorganized KGB. He said that his organization currently lacks the means to fight crime because of the inadequacy of the laws and the corruption among high officials.[62]

The most revealing study to date on illegal diversion of nuclear material was conducted by three Russian investigatory reporters who went looking for the nuclear black market last year. After passing themselves off successfully as prospective buyers, they found at least some evidence of illegal trade:

> Our investigation led us to conclude that stories of nuclear materials crossing formerly Soviet borders by the ton are global myths. We met 28 dealers. All of them traffic primarily in metals, a trade that has a real and stable market. They deal with radioactive elements only from time to time, when there is the possibility of a really profitable deal. Only two of the 28 had succeeded in closing real deals.[63]

All of this evidence suggests that *large-scale* illegal trading in nuclear material does not yet exist, perhaps only because the appropriate buyers have not shown up. Clearly, this situation could change; there is no reason for complacency.

CHAPTER 2

CHERNOBYL: WHAT HAPPENED?

S ince 1986 a great deal of new research has produced deeper understanding of exactly what happened at Chernobyl and the extent of
the damage inflicted upon the land, water, and people in Ukraine and
its neighbors. Over the last two years the European Union alone has
contributed Ecu 14.2 million for sixteen research projects in the
region.[1] Ukraine, Belarus, and Russia have each conducted their own
investigations.

Ukrainian authorities now estimate that up to 8,000 people may
have died as a direct result of exposure to excessive radiation from the
Chernobyl disaster.[2] A recent Russian-American medical survey estimated that a further 12,000 people were badly irradiated.[3] The
Ukrainian minister of the environment puts the figure even higher.
He estimates that the health of two-thirds of Ukraine's 52 million people may have been harmed by the accident.[4] Between twenty thousand and forty thousand cancer deaths are predicted within the
boundaries of the FSU as a consequence of the accident.[5] Estimates of
the future number of cancer cases in Ukraine, Belarus, and Russia
range from five thousand to a hundred thousand cases.[6]

In Ukraine more than 17 million acres of land where 2.6 million
people live have been contaminated with cesium-137 at a radioactivity
level exceeding one curie per square kilometer. There are other large
areas, in Belarus (especially around Gomel) and in Norway, that received
similar high levels of contamination.[7] According to one expert, since the
Chernobyl catastrophe, Belarus has suffered economic losses equivalent to at least ten national annual budgets.[8] This analyst estimated that

there have been more than 2 million victims—as many Belarussians as were killed or injured in the Great Patriotic War (World War II). Noting that 28 percent of Ukraine's annual state budget is spent on Chernobyl matters, he wondered how it would survive in the coming decades.

Until very recently, secrecy concealed the extent to which children had been exposed to dangerous radiation. The Russian Federation's Academy of Medical Sciences has now reported that 50 percent of the children in Bryansk oblast have received excessive doses of 200-plus rads in the five years since the accident. In 1993 researchers at the Biophysics Institute of the Russian Federation Ministry of Health examined five thousand children up to age sixteen who lived within thirty kilometers of the Chernobyl plant (the "Zone of Exclusion") and five hundred persons aged twenty to sixty-one who lived adjacent to the zone at the time of the accident. Many of those studied were found to be suffering from immune system disorders.[9] It is now believed that 50 percent of the children who reside in zones with measurements of at least forty curies per square kilometer of cesium-137 have manifested the primary stages of chronic radiation sickness.[10] Other reports indicate that lymph node increases were found in 90 percent of the children exposed to fallout from the accident. Thirty percent were found to have disturbances of the stomach and digestive tract, and 15 percent disorders of the blood. In Ukraine and Belarus, infantile thyroid gland cancer has increased dramatically, according to a survey by the World Health Organization (WHO).[11] Since 1989 there have been 225 new cases reported in Belarus and 157 reported in Ukraine; normally there would only have been two to three cases between them.[12]

WHY SO MUCH RADIATION?

Recent doctoral research completed by Alexander Sich and by Dr. Alexandr Borovoy, his thesis supervisor in Ukraine and head of the permanent team at Chernobyl, has provided a basis for explaining the new, higher estimates of the number of people irradiated. Sich was the first foreign expert to be given full access to Chernobyl for long-term research. In fact, he is one of the few nuclear engineers of any nationality to be permitted such an opportunity. He spent more than a year and a half at the facility analyzing and reconstructing the Chernobyl accident.

According to Sich, Soviet efforts from the second through the seventh day after the accident to drop 5,000 tons of sand, clay, dolomite, boron carbonate, and lead by helicopter over the burning reactor core were futile. The material never entered the core shaft,[13] therefore these heroic efforts did not succeed, as the Soviets claimed at the time, in cooling, smothering, and sealing the core from the environment and stopping the further release of radionuclides.[14] Sich and Borovoy now believe the core burned unchecked for nine days, releasing at least three times more harmful radiation elements of the seven most significant volatile isotopes than the Soviets admitted in 1986—that is, 150 million curies, give or take 50 million.[15]

Another major reason for the elevated levels of radiation that are now believed to have affected the population around Chernobyl was the apparent decision by the Soviet Hydrometeorology Committee to secretly seed rain clouds after the nuclear accident so that contaminated rainfall would not reach Moscow.[16] One of the immediate results was the contamination of much of the drinking water of Kiev. From a published interview with Dr. Mykhaylo Kuzmenko, chief of the Fresh Water Radioecology Department of the Hydrobiology Institute in Ukraine, one impact of the Chernobyl accident was to increase the content of cesium-137 and strontium-90 in Ukrainian waters by factors of up to 30,000.[17] The Pripyat River, which leads to the Kiev Reservoir, was particularly affected. While radiological readings for the water itself have improved, there is a long-term impact on the silt, which in turn leads to contamination of fish and of plants grown in the areas adjacent to the river. When combined with the considerable chemical pollution in this region, even low levels of radionuclides seriously increase the danger to the population.[18]

"UNSAFE AT ANY LEVEL"

The most terrifying finding to come out of the Chernobyl investigation is the possibility, according to many Western and Russian experts, that such an accident could recur elsewhere in the FSU. According to Sich, the "main cause of the Chernobyl accident (from the technical point of view) was reactor instability," due mainly to design faults of the RBMK-1000 reactor. To a lesser extent, violations of operating procedures were responsible.[19] The fundamental design flaws that now principally are blamed for the Chernobyl accident were described in 1991 by Dr. Hans A. Bethe, a Nobel laureate in physics and a longtime

advocate of nuclear power, in a *New York Times* op-ed article which
makes the case that "it can't happen here":

> The Soviet reactor consists of a large block of graphite, in
> which are embedded about 1,700 tubes containing the ura-
> nium that produces fast neutrons. The tubes are cooled by
> water flowing through them. The graphite slows down the
> neutrons so they can interact with uranium-235, continuing
> the chain reaction, and the water absorbs some of these slow
> neutrons, depressing the chain reaction.
>
> The design of the Chernobyl reactor results in an unfor-
> tunate instability. If, for some reason, the reactor produces
> excess power, more of the cooling water will turn to steam,
> fewer neutrons will be absorbed by water and more of them
> will be absorbed by uranium-235. This increases the already
> too high power still further. That is exactly what happened at
> Chernobyl: The power increased and the reactor became
> uncontrollable.[20]

This key statement in Bethe's report relates to the Soviet design incor-
porating a positive void coefficient, precisely the opposite of what is
found in Western and later Russian reactor designs.

Based on his own research, Sich points to several additional
design problems that figured in the Chernobyl accident: When the
reactor is operated at low power it is extremely difficult, if not impossible, for the operators to monitor exactly what is happening within.
Sich quotes the original report of the Gosatomnadzor on the accident:
"At low power levels a reactor operator has to operate 'blindly,' relying
more on experience and intuition than on the readings of the control
instruments."[21] It was an experimental safety test requiring precisely
such low-power operation of the generator (approximately 6 percent
of full power) that preceded the accident at Chernobyl. The Chernobyl
operators, who lacked both training and explicit procedural guidance,
found their experience and instincts inadequate in the moment of crisis.[22] Furthermore, according to Sich, the time required for inserting
the control rods into the core was "desperately slow" (at twenty seconds), and, critically, one control rod graphite "follower" did not match
the full height of the reactor core.[23] Sich also points to structural defi-
ciencies, including the vulnerability to stress of the zirconium to stain-
less steel transition welds at the inlet and outlet of the fuel pressure

channels in the core.[24] Most importantly, the reactor did not have an adequate containment shell to prevent the escape of radioactive material in case of an accident.[25]

In the view of most Western experts, the Chernobyl reactor was an accident waiting to happen. The overcomplicated system of pipes, release valves, and water cooling functions provided a huge area interface with potential disaster. Each channel and its corresponding system for cooling of steam pipes were prone to excess pressure, which could result in a burst, leakage, or even a steam explosion. Fire protection systems were almost nonexistent, and machinery around the plant was badly outdated and worn. Finally, generators for emergency use needed start-up times of as much as three minutes—in U.S. reactors, ten seconds is considered too long for emergency power—and Soviet safety rules confused operators about the use of backup power.[26]

At the heart of the Chernobyl tragedy, Sich observes, lay an approach to designing safe nuclear reactors that was very different from that of the West:

> The fundamental safety assumption in the West is that mankind's technology will never be "perfect" and, as such, that accidents do occur. Western safety practices and systems are consequently designed with this in mind. Soviet safety policies, on the other hand, were formulated upon the less conservative assumptions regarding the ability of man-made safety systems to prevent a natural physical process from *ever* occurring.[27]

In the West, stability in reactors is based upon physical principles and not on safety systems dependent on quick and proper human response. Western light-water reactors, for example, are designed so that in the event of a loss of cooling water, a physical process slows down the reaction.[28]

CAN SOVIET REACTORS BE MADE SAFE?

Based on a national inventory of nuclear facilities conducted after the Tomsk-7 accident, Gosatomnadzor divides Russian nuclear facilities into two categories.[29] The first category consists of reactors developed and constructed before many of the current revelations about design and maintenance flaws came to light. It includes eleven graphite cooled RBMK-1000 reactors, similar to those at Chernobyl, built between 1973 and 1986. There are four such reactors at Sosnovy Bor (near Leningrad), four at Kursk, and three at Smolensk. (Outside of the Russian Federation only six such RBMK reactors were built: four at Chernobyl in Ukraine and two at Ignalina in Lithuania).[30] Also included in this category are four VVER-440 reactors of the first generation (model V230), which were built between 1956 and 1970. Two are located at Novovoronezh and two at Kola. (Outside of the Russian Federation, two such reactors were built in Armenia, four in Bulgaria, two in the Czech Republic, and four in Germany.[31] The VVER-440 model V230 reactor uses light water to moderate the fission of the fuel; and water is used to cool the reactor.

Gosatomnadzor believes that all reactors in this first category require radical reconstruction because of the repeated failure of obsolete or worn-out equipment and system components. Stress tolerances were inadequately considered, and existing safety procedures no longer conformed to accepted standards.[32] According to the Russian minister of the environment, neither the RBMK nor the VVER-440 can be raised to international standards by retrofitting measures or by introducing state-of-the-art technology.[33] The minister has called for closing down all eleven RBMK reactors in Russia as soon as possible.[34]

By Western standards, both types of reactors (RBMK and VVER-440 model V230) have significant safety problems. Neither reactor has an adequate concrete and metal radiation containment structure in case of a nuclear accident. In the case of VVER-440 model V230 reactors, the Accident Localization System (ALS), which serves as a partial reactor containment, was designed to handle only one four-pipe rupture. In case of a more extensive coolant pipe(s) rupture, the system would vent directly into the atmosphere.[35] However, it is the RBMK (Chernobyl-type) reactor that is the most inadequate and potentially dangerous, largely because it has a "positive void coefficient," which means that the nuclear chain reaction accelerates as the temperature in the reactor rises.[36] At a debate in the European Parliament in May 1992 on the subject of nuclear safety and security, a German expert said of the out-of-date reactors, "Even with refurbishment, the risk is so great that it is likely we will have a serious accident in the next ten years."[37]

Second and third generations of nuclear reactors comprise the second category, and for which Gosatomnadzor believes that many of the problems of the older plants do not exist. Many of the earlier design flaws were corrected in these models such as the VVER-440 model 213 and VVER-1000, which came into service beginning in 1981, and improved monitoring equipment was utilized.[38] Reactors built after 1981 have full containment structures, as in the West.[39]

THE HUMAN ELEMENT

In reports made shortly after the Chernobyl accident, the Soviet government attributed most of the blame to the Chernobyl block 4 operators.[40] Since then, the pronuclear lobby has argued that more modern equipment, better training, and improved procedures would render even the RBMK-type reactor safe. Mykola Sorokin, director of the Chernobyl Atomic Energy Facility, claims that since 1986 the government has made 3,400 engineering or equipment modifications to Chernobyl-type (RBMK) reactors to prevent a repeat accident.

There is no question but that human error played into, that is, compounded, the inherent design faults to cause the Chernobyl catastrophe. It is also clear that a clumsy response by Soviet officials—coupled with the unprecedented nature of the crisis and various initial missteps by plant management—probably made the situation worse. However, a more accurate description of the crisis would be that an accident-prone reactor, serviced by a workforce with less and less reason to be conscientious, within an increasingly dysfunctional bureaucracy, reached its day of reckoning.

On the eve of the accident Chernobyl was a microcosm reflecting all the inherent contradictions and societal pathology of the Soviet state in 1986. Morale was low, labor discipline was poor, and honest work went largely unrewarded. Untruthfulness, speculation, theft, and corruption were widespread. Errors were hidden, mistakes buried. The ruling elite and government bureaucracy were out of touch, focused principally on meeting production quotas and preserving their own privileges.[41]

The 1986 Central Committee report on Chernobyl, released in 1992, found that government officials responsible for the plant and the safety of the community failed to respond in a timely and effective fashion. No concrete plans for an emergency situation of such magnitude had been developed prior to the accident. Sluggish response by local officials in the period immediately after the accident further complicated the problem.[42] Sich reports that the head of the Nuclear

Energy Division of the Ukrainian Ministry of Energy and Electrifi-
cation at the time of the accident told him that no one had any "official" idea what had happened until thirty-six hours after the accident.[43]
Fearing panic might quickly follow, authorities blocked the dissemination of critical information to the general public until it was
too late.

There is no indication that the management and staff of nuclear
plants are any better prepared today. In fact, they may be even less
prepared than previously thought. The *Los Angeles Times* reported in
February 1994 that

> in its first survey as an independent body with enhanced
> powers, the Federal Nuclear and Radiation Safety Oversight
> Committee [Gosatomnadzor] counted 20,000 safety violations
> in 1993—nearly four for each of the 5,500 inspections it made.
> As a result, the agency said it temporarily shut down 78 of
> the 14,500 enterprises involved in atomic power, repri-
> manded 232 officials and charged two others with crimes. It
> also gave pop quizzes on safety procedures to 5,000 atomic
> energy workers and flunked 437 of them.[44]

The article quotes Yuri G. Vishnevskiy, chairman of Gosatomnadzor, who admits that "there are serious drawbacks in the way we
approach the problem of physical safety of nuclear materials in this
country."[45] This first inventory of Russian nuclear power plants indicated that nearly 40 percent of all violations were due to shortcom-
ings in the work of maintenance personnel.[46] Dosimetry and
radiometry devices for measuring the discharge of radioactive substances were not being checked in a timely manner. More than 50 percent of the accessible radiation monitoring equipment in 1992 had
not been checked at all;[47] Gosatomnadzor had not been authorized to
examine military or secret facilities at this point.

There have been numerous accidents, serious and minor, at
Soviet-built nuclear power stations. Some of the worst—or at least the
most widely reported in recent years—include:

- 118 fires at Russian nuclear power plants between 1986 and
  1992, 60 percent of which occurred in the machine and reactor halls. Most of Russia's nuclear power plants are still inadequately protected against fire.[48]

- a breakdown in a regulator valve shutter on one of the water cooling pipes at Sosnovy Bor on March 24, 1992, resulting in the release of radioactivity into the atmosphere. The Estonian government immediately protested to the Russian authorities and demanded that Sosnovy Bor be shut down.[49]

- an oil switch explosion on April 29, 1992, requiring the Balakovo atomic facility to partially shutdown.[50]

- a short circuit in the system for protection against earthquakes of the Khmelnitskiy nuclear station in Ukraine caused by heavy rain on May 31, 1992, which resulted in an automatic power reduction.[51]

- a fault in the measuring systems detected at the South Ukrainian power plant on September 21, 1992, which caused an automatic shutdown. Gosatomnadzor reported that plant workers had "failed to observe the requirements for the safe maintenance of the reactor."[52]

- a condensate tank leak at the Polarnyye Zori station on the Kola Peninsula in Russia on September 12, 1992.[53]

- a fire in the backup electrical equipment at the Kozloduy plant in Bulgaria in late September 1992.[54]

- a radioactive leak at Ignalina in Lithuania on October 15, 1992, which resulted in a shutdown.[55]

- an "intensive leakage of steam from the turbines" at the Kursk atomic energy station in Russia in December 1992, forcing a shutdown. Casualties among staff were reported there.[56]

- two fires at Chernobyl within a forty-eight-hour period in January 1993, one of which took place in a section of the sarcophagus built over the destroyed reactor.[57]

- looseness in the gasket of the safety control systems drive at Khmelnitskiy, which on April 29, 1993, had to be temporarily disconnected from the power grid.[58]

- on November 24, 1993, overheating at the Tver nuclear facility, which was shut down by an automatic security system.[59]

- a leak in the cooling system at Sosnovy Bor on February 22, 1994, which forced the shutdown of one reactor.[60]

- a fire in a machine room adjacent to the reactor at Khmelnitskiy in March 1994.[61]

AN ECONOMIC AND SOCIAL CRISIS

The collapse of the old command economy, and the lack of an effective market system to replace it, has left the power industry, and particularly the nuclear facilities, in a dangerous economic limbo. The minister of fuel and energy estimated that by early 1993 the Russian energy sector was owed 1.8 trillion rubles by its customers, and it in turn owed 1.1 trillion rubles to its suppliers.[62] The Russian and Ukrainian nuclear industry reportedly has a combined debt of 104 billion rubles (including a 16.5 billion-ruble debt owed by nuclear plants in Ukraine) to TVEL, an umbrella company of nuclear fuel manufacturers administered by the Ministry of Atomic Energy.[63] The nuclear industry is owed 350 to 450 billion rubles by its consumers; it has been able to collect less than 17 percent of its operating expenses. Under these kinds of constraints, "hundreds of nuclear electric power stations are unable to acquire fuel or carry out current repairs."[64] Because of the financial crisis, Leonid Proskuryakov, the general director of TVEL, warned in July 1994 that the entire atomic energy industry, including its weapons complex, may come to a halt.[65]

In February 1994, the staff of the Bilibino nuclear power plant in Russia's Magadan region decided to suspend two generating units and considered suspending the two remaining ones when a lack of funds prevented payment for further fuel supplies.[66] Sources indicated that the plant was owed eight billion rubles by its customers, mainly gold mining firms. It owed seven billion rubles to its own suppliers.[67] Workers' salaries had not been paid since the previous December.[68] Families of many specialists were reported to be "on the brink of starvation."[69] This kind of situation appears to be widespread. At Kola there was a threatened shutdown of all reactors in April 1993 because only 9 percent of the power supplied had been paid for by consumers.[70] At Chernobyl, 20 percent of the key technical staff—presumably searching for better-paying jobs—departed in 1993, which must have set back efforts to ensure safety at the facility.[71]

In June 1994 scientists at Chelyabinsk-70 publicly appealed for assistance, noting that inadequate and tardy funding had brought the plant to a "critical point."[72] Requests to central authorities for aid generally went unanswered. The enterprise owed billions of rubles to suppliers, the equipment was aging, and there was a shortage of materials, instruments, and special work clothing. The plant's suppliers of gas and electricity were threatening to cut off energy. There were no funds for health care, housing construction had ceased, and families with children were being forced to live in dormitories. The scientists warned of the increased risk of reactor emergency arising if immediate action were not taken.

The monetary difficulties of the nuclear industry are not, of course, unique; they directly related to the crisis confronting all state industries of the FSU. The huge, bankrupt state enterprises are the main clients of the various nuclear power plants, and their indebtedness is the principal cause of the financial straits in which most nuclear power plants now find themselves. However, the atomic industry faces a special problem: In other industries difficulties in meeting payrolls, fuel bills, and equipment costs plus shoddy maintenance, deteriorating equipment, and growing plant theft are worrisome; in the case of the nuclear power stations, they are a potential catastrophe.

Another major difference exists between the nuclear industry and other state enterprises. Theoretically, the government has the option of simply closing down most state-run factories; with the nuclear industry the situation is much more complicated because of technical difficulties in shutting down a reactor. It is not possible to throw a switch and tell the last worker out to close the plant door; rather, the process is complicated, time-consuming, costly, and potentially dangerous if not executed correctly. At Chernobyl, when there were calls for closing down all remaining RBMK generators in operation, plant technicians warned that it would take ten years and cost $6–8 billion to implement the shutdown.[73] After a nuclear plant has ceased functioning, it continues to require energy and personnel to maintain safety. This, in fact, happened when the Armenian atom plant was shut down after the earthquake in 1986, and the continuing maintenance cost is one of the major arguments for resuming operation.

It is in the context of the overall financial crisis, with declining budgets and plummeting morale, that the lessons of Chernobyl seem most worrisome and the need for Western action becomes most urgent.

CHAPTER 3

THE THREAT TO THE ARCTIC OCEAN
AND THE JAPAN AND BALTIC SEAS

Ecocide in the USSR described a belt of heavy radiation pollution in the north stretching from Arkhangel'sk to Murmansk. New evidence, including reports of radioactive contamination of caribou in northwest Alaska and allegedly irradiated migratory ducks (also from Alaska) on Long Island, has confirmed the widespread ecological damage caused by nuclear testing, radioactive dumping, and nuclear accidents in Russia.[1] Today radiation pollution primarily threatens the Arctic Ocean and the Sea of Japan as well as the Baltic Sea.

From August 1949 to December 1987, 618 known nuclear explosions were conducted on the territory of Soviet Union.[2] Of these, 118 were conducted at Novaya Zemlya in the Arctic.[3] Of the 618 known tests, 108 explosions were considered "peaceful," that is, conducted for economic purposes. It is estimated that fifty such peaceful explosions were conducted in the Arctic region.[4] At least three tests were conducted underwater in the Arctic region—one in the Barents Sea in 1955 and two off the coast of Novaya Zemlya in 1957 and in 1961.[5]

Additional research conducted by a Committee of Inquiry on nuclear waste dumping along Russia's Arctic and Pacific shores obtained some alarming results. Under Alexey Yablokov's direction, the study was carried out by the nuclear and health inspectorates, the military, and other agencies involved in dumping activities. The remarkably frank report presented to President Yeltsin gave the precise

43

location of past radioactive dumping, including that of waste from nuclear-powered submarines. An analysis of the report in the *Observer* (London) revealed that dumping had taken place in the Kara Sea, the Bering Sea, and the Sea of Japan.[6] Since 1965 twenty nuclear reactors have been dumped (some with their fuel rods still intact) from ten nuclear submarines and the icebreaker Lenin. Nine reactors (four still with their fuel rods) lie in Arctic waters only twenty meters (sixty feet) deep.

THE KOMSOMOLETS

The Yablokov Arctic study also warned of imminent danger from the nuclear submarine *Komsomolets*, which sank three hundred miles off the Norwegian coast in 1989. The committee warned that the two nuclear warheads and the reactor on board are corroding, and that by 1996–97 there will be an "uncontrolled" and "impulsive" leak of plutonium that could poison plankton and destroy the rich fishing waters.[7]

In reality, contradictory conclusions were promulgated by military and environmental commentators about the prospect for quick release of toxic radioactive material from the *Komsomolets*. If nuclear materials were released slowly, the toxicity would be rendered largely harmless by the movement of the seas. However, if a quick release occurs, the health of adjacent populations will be endangered as the contaminants work their way through the food chain. Moreover, the level of danger posed by leaking plutonium could depend on the time of the year. According to Igor D. Spassky, vice-chairman of the Komsomolets Foundation and director of the Rubin Marine Engineering Bureau, if the leakage occurred in the summer, when plankton are near the ocean surface, plutonium most likely would not contaminate the microorganisms and would instead drop to the ocean floor. However, if the leak occurred in the winter, when plankton feed at lower depths, there could be more danger to the lower end of the food chain.[8]

Thus, there is much uncertainty about how great a priority should be assigned to the problem. The Norwegian government seems to be little threatened by the *Komsomolets* nuclear submarine, although the vessel was sunk off its coast, because it is located at a depth of 5,000 feet. Spokesmen for the Norwegian government have disagreed with the view that the submarine poses an ecological threat, contending that more damage could be caused by attempting to raise it.[9] Yet if radioactive leakage results in penetration of the food chain, one Russian expert figured that Russian fishing losses could amount to some $2 million and Norwegian losses up to $2 billion.[10]

An estimate of the cost of raising the *Komsomolets* was set at $250 million, but it might not be possible because the submarine is so badly damaged. Dr. Kathleen Crane, a scholar from Columbia University working on the Arctic region with the Naval Research Laboratory in Washington, D.C., has expressed the fear shared by many experts that bad weather and sea conditions in the vicinity of the *Komsomolets* (locally called the "corridor of hell") could cause great difficulties in salvaging the submarine.[11] A mid-1994 evaluation by the Russian government provided a less apocalyptic assessment. Nonetheless, certain measures to seal rather than raise the submarine were taken. In late June 1994 the Russians commenced securing the *Komsomolets* with cement, and by the first week of August 1994 the work was completed.[12] As a result, experts now believe that the sunken submarine will no longer pose a danger to the sea and its marine life.

THE NORTHERN FLEET

Unfortunately, past nuclear tests, the dumping of nuclear waste off the Arctic and Pacific coasts, and the sunken *Komsomolets* do not represent the only radioactive threat to these bodies of water. A greater danger may come from continuing efforts to operate the Russian nuclear-powered fleet and to dismantle decommissioned, aging nuclear vessels.

According to a study by the Bellona Foundation of Norway, which has been active in following environmental issues in Russia since the 1990s, there are 182 working nuclear reactors in the region of Arkhangel'sk-Murmansk, as well as another 135 reactors that have ceased operation.[13] The authors report that significant amounts of radioactive waste are stored at fifteen different locations in the region,[14] and they go on to note that radioactive dumping in this area constitutes two-thirds of all radioactive materials ever dumped in all the oceans of the world.

Following the Tomsk-7 accident, President Yeltsin established an interdepartmental commission to investigate radiation safety problems related to nuclear power facilities and equipment in the Russian Navy's Northern Fleet. Results of the investigation demonstrated that the overwhelming majority of the Northern Fleet's facilities and equipment was in a "catastrophic" state.[15] The commission cited flagrant

violations of safety rules with almost no efforts at remedial actions,
warning that nuclear power plants were being operated by the "poke
method," a descriptive term suggesting untrained and unscientific
methods of operation. It further expressed a serious concern over the
navy's handling of radioactive waste. Reportedly, Russia has 235 ships
with nuclear reactors on board, 228 of them military ships and 7 "civilian." In all there are 394 nuclear reactors on board navy ships and 12
reactors on board icebreakers. According to a Radio Free Europe/Radio
Liberty summary from June 1993, these figures represent 60 percent of
the world's total number of reactors. This contributes to a secondary
problem, an abundance of waste—20,000 cubic meters of radioactive
liquid waste and 6,000 tons of solid waste—the by-products of the
tremendous amount of fuel that these reactors require to operate. For
example, in order for one reactor in a nuclear submarine to operate
with properly enriched uranium, it takes about 75 tons of uranium
ore, 99.8 percent of which becomes waste.[16] After a period of time,
these wastes will exact a tremendous cost in terms of both money and
the land repositories in which to store the waste. In fact, radioactive
waste tanks have been found to be overflowing, yet the Russian navy
was undertaking no efforts at cleanup nor was it indicating any need
for outside help.

The Ministry of Atomic Energy now admits that radioactive waste
has been (and continues to be) stored in floating tankers in northern
ports such as Arkhangel'sk and in the fjords of the Kola Peninsula and
the Far East and that removing the radioactive waste from the ships is
"an exercise which will cost enormous sums. Unfortunately, these
ships are in a state which they cannot be towed out into the open
sea."[17] The deteriorated tankers are filled to capacity.

According to Yevgeny Stomatyuk, chairman of the Far East
Territorial Committee on Natural Resources, at the time action was
finally taken, the TNT-5 (nuclear waste tanker) used in the Far East
had only one to one-and-one-half months remaining before a real
catastrophe was likely to occur. Although the waste was ultimately
transferred from the tankers in the Far East, the principal concerns
about radioactive toxic waste storage and dumping elsewhere remain.

Removing the remaining waste from the ships will cost an enormous sum. In addition, the navy normally refuels twenty submarine
reactors each year but only has storage space for spent fuel from three
reactors, according to the report commissioned by President Yeltsin.[18]
Responding to Japanese and other protests about the dumping, Dr.

Viktor Danilov-Danilyan, the Russian minister of environment, indicated that it might be possible to build appropriate new waste storage facilities, given at least three years and $10 million. In the meantime, he warned, the Russians might have to resume dumping at sea.[19]

Russia's aging nuclear fleet is a potential time bomb for both the Arctic Ocean and the Sea of Japan. Information released since the *Komsomolets* sank in 1987 has reinforced Western suspicions that early Soviet nuclear submarines suffered from continual problems, which persist even today.[10] The Bellona and Komsomolets foundations cite more than fifty "serious accidents" during the operation and maintenance of the nuclear submarines of the Northern Fleet.[21] From 1989 to 1993 alone there were ten accidents of various types on nuclear submarines and at Northern Fleet bases.[22] In addition to the sinking of the *Komsomolets*, four of the most serious recent accidents include:

- An emergency on a nuclear submarine in July 1989, when cracks appeared in the casing for the reactor's cooling system;

- Two fires aboard a nuclear submarine moored at Severodvinsk in December 1990;

- A fire aboard a submarine in the Barents Sea in May 1992; and

- Two fires on Northern Fleet submarines as recently as 1993.[23]

The Russian Navy has itself recognized that its antiquated nuclear submarines—most of which are over twenty years old—represent a danger. Its commander-in-chief, Admiral Feliks Gromov, announced in 1993 that eighty outdated nuclear submarines had been "decommissioned" and that one-third of them had had their reactors removed.[24] According to Joshua Handler of Greenpeace, there are approximately 120 Russian submarines now out of service or on the verge of going out of service. Approximately forty to fifty of these nuclear-powered submarines are in the Far East, with facilities mainly around the Shkotovo and Kamchatka Peninsulas. The remaining submarines are in the North, spread between bases on the Kola Peninsula and at Severodvinsk.[25]

The decision to decommission eighty nuclear submarines—and possibly half again as many—is welcome; however, it is not without certain dangers. Removing nuclear fuel (or refueling) is a complicated and sometimes dangerous process; accidents have happened. One of the worst took place August 1985 at the Chazhma Ship Repair Facility on the south side of Chazhma Bay, approximately forty-five kilometers southeast of Vladivostok on the Shkotovo Peninsula. A reactor on an "Echo-II" SSGN vessel exploded at the end of a refueling operation, radioactively contaminating the surrounding land and sea.[26] Consider the peril to the harbor communities where these ships congregate; at Severodvinsk alone, according to the mayor, the amount of radioactive material on nuclear submarines berthed inside the city is twenty times greater than in Unit Four at Chernobyl.[27]

If decommissioning nuclear vessels is a complicated and dangerous task at the best of times, these are not the best of times for the Russian Navy. The military, like all other government agencies, is facing difficult budgetary constraints. Yablokov has claimed that there is not even adequate funding to take the Northern Fleet out to sea on exercises.[28]

ADDITIONAL SOURCES OF RADIOACTIVE CONTAMINATION

Russian nuclear facilities—including unsafe reactors—located outside the territory of the Far North represent yet another significant threat to the Arctic Ocean. The principal place of concern is Mayak (alternatively called Chelyabinsk-40 and later Chelyabinsk-65). Uncontained dumping of radioactive waste into the Techa River from 1949 to 1952, as well as radiation from an accident in 1957 and a dumping accident in 1967 at Lake Karachay, and ultimately into the Arctic Ocean, have all resulted in recordings of six hundred microroentgens per hour (the normal background radiation rate would be approximately ten to twelve microroentgens per hour). Cumulative radioactivity at the site, owing to the processing of weapons-grade plutonium at the Mayak Production Association, now exceeds one billion curies; 120 million curies are in holding ponds. As a result of all of these actions, radioactive elements now are penetrating the northern river basins, especially the Ob River.

U.S. territory has already been endangered by Soviet radioactive dumping in the Arctic Ocean and by the belt of radiation that stretches from Arkhangel'sk to Murmansk. Former director of the Central Intelligence Agency Robert N. Gates testified in August 1992 at hearings of the U.S. Senate Intelligence Committee held in Fairbanks, Alaska, that radioactivity from Chelyabinsk and other remote sites profoundly affects the entire north.[29] According to Gates, waste from contaminated watersheds, such as the Techa River, "reportedly was discovered in the Arctic as early as 1951."[30]

NONRADIOACTIVE CONTAMINATION

Radioactive waste is not the only pollution threat in the Arctic Ocean. Ordinary industrial waste, including hazardous materials, has been found from the northern coast of Russia to coasts of Alaska and Canada. A preliminary map of PCB and DDT contamination detected in these waters was published in the *Washington Post* on May 17, 1993.[31] Dr. Kathleen Crane, then working for the Environmental Defense Fund, described the accumulation of PCBs and DDT in the Arctic Ocean to the U.S. Interagency Arctic Research Policy Committee in May 1993. Her report indicated that

> organochlorines and heavy metals have accumulated in some cases, at toxic levels, around the margins of the Arctic Ocean, on neighboring land masses, in fresh and salt water and in the plants and animals who inhabit or visit this region. . . . Preliminary data . . . show the highest concentrations of contaminants in Eurasia and along its shores. Elevated levels of PCBs, DDT, HCH and heavy metals are also observed in the central Arctic Ocean and reach the shores of Canada, Greenland and Svalbard, indicating a very long-range transport.[32]

THREATS TO PARTICULAR SEAS

THE SEA OF OKHOTSK

The Sea of Okhotsk, in the Far East, presents a special problem, as well as an opportunity in terms of pollution cleanup and resource management. Oil pollution in this sea, which has supplied about twenty percent of Russia's fish catch, must be decontaminated as soon as possible before any fish can be caught at all. Recent Western discoveries using bioremediation techniques (releasing bacteria to digest petroleum) may be sufficient for the purpose. Soviet experiments in the field of bacterial controls began much earlier than in the West, but this early work appears to have been unappreciated, undervalued, and underfunded. Internationally funded joint research projects at this point might produce new, effective approaches to bioremediation.

In the interim, in order to protect the remaining fish, the Russian Parliament enacted an ordinance effective June 15, 1993, prohibiting fishing by Russian and foreign vessels in the central region of the sea, which Russia asserts to be its exclusive economic zone.[33] Parliament acted, pending an international agreement, to stop "fishermen operating in a predatory manner destroying valuable biological resources." It remains to be seen how effective this ordinance will be in restraining fishing by nationals of other countries. Given the rise in nationalistic feelings after the elections of December 1993, the Russian government undoubtedly will be more alert to infringements of its territory and food supply.

THE BALTIC SEA

After the Aral Sea, the Baltic poses the greatest difficulty in regard to pollution. The major threats here are from chemical weapons and potential nuclear waste leakage from holding ponds. For years it has been known that after World War II the allied powers dumped considerable amounts of chemical weapons into the Baltic Sea. However, outside of the four countries of Scandinavia (Denmark, Norway, Sweden, and Finland), the three Baltic countries (Estonia, Latvia, and Lithuania), and the remaining three members of the Baltic Sea Convention (Poland, Germany, and Russia), minimal attention is paid to the potential chemical contamination of the entire Baltic region.[34] In 1992 a *Sunday Times Magazine* (London) article reported that, soon after the end of World War II, the Allies deposited more than 250,000 tons of captured chemical weapons materials from Germany and 50,000 tons of their own stocks into the Baltic Sea, the North Sea, and the Skagerrak off the northern tip of Denmark.[35] At least 200,000 tons of chemical weapons found by the Americans and the British were dumped at various sites off the coasts of Scandinavia. The article quoted a British medical officer, Dr. Stephen Musgrave, to the effect that stockpiled poison gases were collected and transported from Emden and Kiel in Germany and then quietly dumped into the Skagerrak. Ships loaded with canisters of chemical weapons materials were scuttled at three sites in this region—in the depths near Arendal, Norway, near the Swedish port of Lysekil, and off Bornholm Island in northern Denmark. A fourth site was located in the Lille Bält, between the Danish island Fyn and the mainland.

Soviet chemical weapons dumping also became a heated issue with the publication of this *Sunday Times Magazine* article. Two Russian participants at the 43d Pugwash Conference in June 1993 confirmed that during the latter part of 1945 and throughout 1946, the Soviets collected from the German chemical arsenal

> About 35,000 tons of chemical weapons, including 408,565 shells, 71,469 aerial 250-kg bombs with mustard gas, 17,000 bombs with adamsite and other arsenic containing CW agents, 1,004 containers (of 1.5 ton capacity each) with mustard gas, 10,420 chemical mines and 7,860 vessels with "cyclon" poison. According to the two scientists, Soviet military personnel abandoned initial plans to dump these materials into the depths of the Atlantic Ocean and dumped them into the shallow waters of the Baltic Sea instead, at two sites south of the Swedish island of Gotland and east of the Danish island of Bornholm.[36]

Former Stasi (state security) archives indicate that the (East) German Democratic Republic authorities also dumped poison gas near Bornholm Island. Other sources stipulate that chemical weapons stocks were dumped near the seaport of Liepaja in Latvia, which is close to the border of Lithuania.[37]

In addition, near the Baltic Sea allegedly are "seventeen underground storage facilities 'inherited' from the German Army in 1945 . . . located on the territory of the Russian Baltic Fleet arsenal. There are 100–150 carloads of different munitions. . . . Their condition is frightening."[38] The author, I. Rudnikov, speculates that some of the chemical weapons materials thought to be in the Baltic Sea are actually in these underground facilities.

The latest revelations about Soviet dumping in the Baltic Sea indicate that there are not 30,000 to 40,000 tons of World War II chemical weapons, as revealed previously, but 400,000 tons or more of various hazardous substances.[39] Thus, toxic chemicals pose an even larger ecological danger to the Baltic than formerly thought. The problem, however, may be mitigated by slow leakage of the containers as the contents are gradually exposed to the sea's natural hydrolyzing process. But if most of the containers leak simultaneously and in significant quantities, the normal diluting processes may be overwhelmed, resulting in a major environmental hazard for the populations of the Baltic Sea region. Some materials, such as mustard gas and adamsite, cannot be hydrolyzed quickly, if at all, and present a real danger to the biosphere.

THE GULF OF FINLAND

Located in Estonia only sixty feet from the Gulf of Finland, which feeds directly into the Baltic Sea, is a radioactive toxic waste dump sixty feet deep and two miles wide that acts as the holding pond for the nearby Sillamäe Uranium Ore Concentration Plant. It is open to the air and separated from the sea by an earthen dam.[40] The dam's embankment is a mere thirty feet wide and sixty feet high. This artificial lake is located in a formerly closed Soviet military city ninety kilometers (fifty-five miles) east of Tallinn, near the Russian border. This toxic waste site threatens the entire Baltic Sea region. If the dam bursts or has a major leak, massive amounts of low- and middle-level radioactive waste could be released into the gulf and then the Baltic Sea. Through September 1992, at least, the Estonians had not been able to investigate this closed city. But a ten-member international investigative team (three from Sweden, four from Finland, and three from Estonia) analyzed the contents of the Sillamäe toxic waste depository in 1993. This team, whose report was cited in a newspaper article by Raimo Mustonen of the Finnish Radiation and Atomic Regulatory Center,[41] found 4,000,000 tons of uranium ore waste, 1,500,000 tons of oil shale ash, 200,000 tons of calcium fluoride, 1,200 tons of uranium, and 800 tons of thorium.

According to this report, waste products from twenty-seven heavy metals were also found. Radium in the depository was recorded at one thousand times the natural environmental background level; uranium at one hundred times, while zinc, copper, aluminum, chrome, lead, phosphorus, nickel, and other materials all registered at more than one hundred times natural readings. Another source indicates that there may also be as much as one thousand tons of radium, and about three hundred thousand tons of calcium sulfate,[42] or as little as eight kilograms of radium.[43] Regardless of the precise amounts, these sites constitute a clear and present danger to vast numbers of people in and around the former Soviet Union.

CHAPTER 4

DYING LAKES, RIVERS, AND INLAND SEAS

In 1989 official Russian sources indicated that three-quarters of all surface water in the Soviet Union was polluted.[1] Even after treatment only half of the water was believed to be drinkable. In addition, most seas, rivers, and lakes were found to be in danger of dying of eutrophication (oxygen deprivation), thus threatening the livelihood of adjacent populations. The information on water pollution, however, remains incomplete. The Russian government intends to expand testing of all surface and subsurface waters. Officials admit that their current knowledge of the extent of water pollution and the nature of the specific pollutants is fragmentary and minimal.

At present, it is estimated that half of all the populated settlements in Russia, including some of the most densely populated cities, consume polluted surface water.[2] In addition to the radioactive dumping mentioned in the previous chapters, there is evidence of widespread discharge of heavy metals, chemical compounds, and various other toxic materials into Russia's rivers, lakes, and seas. It is the mixture of radioactive, industrial, and agricultural wastes in combination with other hazards that has created a particularly dangerous situation for the Russian population, one that Russian medical authorities now fear could cause havoc in genetic inheritance. The government's response to this water crisis has been minimal and may have even weakened since 1992, as the state of the economy, budgetary constraints, and ethnic conflicts have diverted attention and resources from environmental and health tasks.[3] The Russian and other governments of the FSU simply lack the resources for a broad, coordinated attack to eliminate toxic dumping and water pollution.

The Rio Summit on global ecology in June 1993 served as a stimulus for government environmental agencies to evaluate the types and amounts of pollutants in surface waters. The resulting reports, in addition to other studies, have revealed the depth and extent of the water pollution problem in Russia and elsewhere in the FSU:

- In 1988, the Soviet Union was only able to treat 30 percent of the sewage that did not meet sanitary norms. Another 50 percent was improperly purified, and the remaining 20 percent was dumped into the environment untreated.[4]

- The percentage by which certain elements exceeded Maximum Allowable Concentration (PDK, in Russian) levels in surface waters of the Soviet Union in 1991 was staggering: copper compounds, 72–75 percent; phenols, 46–60 percent; petroleum products, 40–49 percent; organic substances, 30–37 percent; zinc, 34–36 percent; nitric acid, 28–43 percent; and ammonia acid, 30–39 percent.[5]

- One-quarter of the water supplied to Russian residences and one-third of the water supplied to institutions in 1991 was "insufficiently cleaned."[6]

- Over the first eight months of 1992, dysentery increased by 50 percent in all of Russia.[7]

- In Moscow, about 45 percent of water and sewage treatment plants surveyed in 1993 were ineffective or malfunctioning, according to the Moscow Environmental Protection Committee.[8]

- Illegal dumping by individuals, military enterprises, industry, and agriculture remains widespread. Most, if not all, of this dumping is excluded from the statistics of water pollution.

- Accidents, leaks, substandard taps, and poor maintenance of waste delivery systems are common problems in Moscow and elsewhere. All pipes, including Moscow's water conduits, were installed without linings, have not been maintained, and are now rotting.

- Between five hundred to seven hundred major accidents have been recorded every year at industrial, petrochemical, agro-chemical, energy, pulp and paper, and other enterprises, generating pollution one hundred times higher than the PDK limits.[9]

- In Moscow, St. Petersburg, Riga, and Vilnius, all of Turkmenistan, and probably other locales throughout the FSU, wastewater treatment plants are insufficient and inadequate, if they exist or are functioning at all.

- The Moscow municipal water purification devices reportedly could be out of service in two years if hard currency is not found to replace existing pumps.

- Most wastewater treatment facilities designs date from the 1950s and 1960s and are not capable of handling oil, radio-active substances, or acids. They also cannot handle chlorine when used as a disinfectant. When combined with organic substances, chlorine forms a dangerous dioxin or other toxic compounds.

This is merely a short selection of the many water-related issues that demand immediate attention.

THE ARAL SEA

The Aral Sea ranks as one of the world's worst ecological catastrophes, affecting not only the immediate region but also undermining the health of populations in remote regions. Dust and salt storms from the region affect the climate from India to the northern regions of Russia.

Until 1960 the Aral Sea was the world's fourth-largest inland body of water. Over the three and a half decades since then the Aral has lost more than 50 percent of its surface area, declining from 67,000 square kilometers in 1960 to less than 34,000 in 1990.[10] As a result, what used to be a highly productive source of fish is virtually dead.

Fishing villages such as Muynak that used to border the Aral Sea are now stranded on a dried-up sea bed sixty kilometers (37 miles) from the new waterfront. About 200,000 square kilometers of what used to be the bottom have been turned into a salt desert. Annually, as much as seventy-five tons of salt, dust, and sand is lifted hundreds of kilometers into the air. The salinity of the Aral Sea has tripled to more than thirty grams per liter of water.[11] The sea itself has separated into two distinct sections, with the larger section splitting further into western and eastern halves.

The direct cause of the desiccation was the diversion of the waters of the Amu-Darya and Syr-Darya rivers, which are the primary feeders of the Aral Sea,[12] to the cotton fields of Uzbekistan and Turkmenistan. This problem was exacerbated by the unsuitability of the infrastructure—the canal through which the diverted waters crossed the Kara-kum desert was almost totally unlined. En route, incredible amounts of water were absorbed into the desert or evaporated; consequently, only 20 to 30 percent of the diverted water reached its destination.[13] Complete lining of the canal would reduce the seepage and would provide more water for the cotton fields; however, the lining itself cannot be installed without the permission of competent local authorities. Local officials, however, continue to deny the significance of such leakage.[14]

The health of the population in the Aral Sea basin has deteriorated frightfully through a combination of the drop in water level, the subsequent release of salt, dust, and sand into the food chain, and water pollution from the utilization of fertilizers, herbicides, and pesticides to improve the fertility of the lands surrounding the sea.

For example, two-thirds of the population in the Kara-kalpak region have cancer of the digestive system, typhoid, or hepatitis. Infant mortality is at least 110 per 1,000 live births. New mothers are advised not to nurse their children because without exception all carry pesticides in their breast milk.[15] Life expectancy is twenty or more years below the national average of the Soviet Union prior to its breakup.[16] Kakimbekk Salykov, the former head of the Committee on Ecology of the USSR Supreme Soviet, said that "academics will never know how bad the situation is; it is worse" than anyone could imagine. Ecocidal policies have resulted in the creation of a situation of extremely high levels of death and illness unequaled in the rest of world. This is a problem for the global environment that will not go away in the near future.

THE BLACK SEA AND THE SEA OF AZOV

The Black Sea is dying. Only 10 percent of its near-surface volume contains oxygen, mainly as a result of large-scale industrial pollution.[17] The Danube, the Don, and the Dnepr rivers, as well as the South Bug River, contribute massive amounts of pollutants. There has been a significant buildup of hydrogen sulfide.

The newspaper *Kiyevskiye vedomosti* reports that there are more than fourteen tons of mercury in the Black Sea, concentrated especially near Yalta and Sevastopol. The Southern Seas Biology Institute of Ukraine estimates that the Black Sea also contains 565,000 tons of mineral nitrogen, 55,000 tons of mineral phosphorus, 206,000 tons of oil, 4,590,000 tons of iron, 1,700 tons of arsenic, and 900 tons of cadmium. In all, some 1,500 different substances have been traced. Pollution levels may be even higher than estimated because Crimean sanitary inspection stations apparently are capable of identifying only one-tenth of the substances present.[18]

One of the economic consequences of this pollution is the reduction of the annual fish catch by two-thirds in a recent seven-year period. (In 1985, 1.5 million tons of fish were caught; in 1992, 500,000 tons.) According to a June 1994 article on the Black Sea that appeared in the *Washington Post,* the catch has now plummeted to 100,000 tons per year.[19] The article further reports that only five species of fish remain out of the twenty-six that could be caught in the Black Sea in the 1960s. Mackerel, previously the backbone of the local fishing industry, has not been fished commercially since 1965. Where once a million dolphin lived, now only 200,000 survive. As for marine mammals, the rare Monk seal has completely vanished. In April 1992, the realities of the situation were already clear enough to alarm the governments of the region—Romania, Bulgaria, Ukraine, Russia, Georgia, and Turkey— and to compel them to sign an international cooperation agreement to try to stop the pollution in the sea.[20]

The six countries met again in 1993 to adopt a declaration that incorporated specific measures to deal with the pollution.[21] The agreement included coordinating development of national plans for reducing emissions of harmful substances and eliminating emergency cases by 1996. Low-waste and waste-free technologies were to be introduced where possible. In addition, countries were prohibited from dumping radioactive materials into the Black Sea. Finally, there were provisions to expand protected territories along the coasts of the Black Sea.

Another body of water that has not received much attention to date is the Sea of Azov, which empties into the Black Sea. The Sea of Azov has been badly contaminated with pesticides in recent years. According to an article published in early 1990 by the World Health Organization, the mean annual concentration of all pesticides in the sea more than quintupled in the period from 1983 to 1987.[22] The author, then head of the Laboratory of the Institute of Fresh Water Biology, asserted that by 1988 the concentration of stable organochlorine pesticides alone had increased by a factor of seventeen compared with the base year of 1983.

THE CASPIAN SEA

If the Sea of Azov is badly polluted with pesticides, the Caspian Sea is worse. According to the submission by the USSR Ministry of Ecology to the Rio Conference, the Sea of Azov contained 7 milligrams of pesticides per liter of water, while the Caspian Sea (northern section) had a long-term average of 44 milligrams per liter, with the current annual average of readings for pesticide contamination ranging from 7 up to 143 milligrams per liter.[23] At the International Conference on the Problems of the Caspian held in 1992 in Baku, pollution was particularly salient because the concentration of oil products and phenols off the coast of Azerbaijan is four to six times the PDK in its northern section, and ten to sixteen times the PDK along Turkmenistan's shoreline.

Determining the pollution levels of the Caspian Sea has become complicated by the recent rise in the level of the sea. By 1993, the Caspian had risen by 214 centimeters over its long-term average level owing to natural causes as well as the closure in 1977 of the canal between the Caspian and the Kara-Bogaz-Gol (a neighboring, small body of water). Potential economic and social losses are enormous. If emergency measures are not taken, at least 4 cities and 109 villages with a total population of 197,000, 2.6 million acres, and 750 miles of electrical power lines on the Caspian coast will be destroyed by the advancing sea of water.[24] According to the director of the Caspian Sea Ecology Laboratory of the Institute of Deserts in Turkmenistan, "Entire areas of coastal territories have been inundated, among them promising gas-bearing areas, agricultural lands, economic sites, and points of settlements in Turkmenistan, Kazakhstan, Azerbaijan, Russia, and Iran."[25]

Costs of the cleanup of pollutants will be ever larger if nothing is done soon. A proposal to dig a canal from the Caspian to provide water for the Aral Sea seems excessively costly in terms of money as well as time, but many of the proposals put forth to resolve this problem follow similar schemes. A number of practical and political issues complicate the problem, including where to find the necessary funds, how to apportion the international burden, and what to do about the ongoing Armenia-Azerbaijan conflict, which continues to divert attention from environmental cooperation.

LAKE BAIKAL

This lake, the world's deepest, has received much global attention because it holds one-fifth of the planet's fresh water and because it has a unique biology. Numerous studies already have been conducted about the causes of its contamination; therefore, it probably will not require additional lengthy analysis before incremental funding can be appropriated to expedite the cleanup of effluents from pulp and paper industry pollution, or from the three hundred or so unfiltered feeder rivers. The apparent decision of the World Bank to grant a $110 million loan ($45 million of which is grant aid) for conservation projects in Russia and particularly for the Lake Baikal region should be an important first step in launching a major international effort to save the lake.[26]

New information indicates that the catchment area may also be contaminated with radioactivity. Local KGB authorities revealed in 1993 that two underground nuclear explosions took place a decade earlier (1982) in Ust-Orda and Ust-Kut, near the lake. Ground radioactivity from those explosions is found even today.[27] A senior Russian official hinted to me that an area to the northeast of Lake Baikal may have worse radioactive contamination than either Chelyabinsk or Chernobyl. It could seriously complicate the "standard" cleanup efforts going on at Lake Baikal if this area is in fact heavily contaminated with radioactive nucleides.

LAKE LADOGA

Lake Ladoga near St. Petersburg is the largest freshwater lake in Europe. Due to well-known and oft-repeated improper storage of fertilizers, soil erosion, and livestock waste, Ladoga has become highly polluted. Cleanup of this lake could serve as an example for other regions with similar patterns of uncontrolled but preventable pollution from similar agricultural activities.

Discovery of containers with radioactive waste materials on an old military ship docked at an island in the lake has engendered concerns about possible other, still unknown secret activities that could lead to further pollution. Insufficient information renders further recommendations for what needs to be done impossible at the present time. Here, as elsewhere in the FSU, one encounters the standard pattern of secrecy about military related activities that hides both present and potential future environmental health problems.

LAKE SEVAN

This lake in Armenia is in danger of disappearing. Earthquakes and war have created an energy shortage in the newly independent republic, and the desperate search for new sources has led to extensive deforestation. Withdrawal of water from Lake Sevan for hydroelectric power facilities has been increased to substitute for the power supply no longer coming from Medzamor, the local atomic power plant (AES) closed after an earthquake because of damage and safety concerns. The process of extracting large quantities of water for hydroelectric plants has begun to threaten the lake's ecology.

It will be necessary either to retrofit the AES (as has been done in California) to withstand a level-nine Richter scale earthquake or to find energy substitutes, such as gas turbines, immediately. If Lake Sevan's water is drawn down further, the impact on the ecosystem may be permanent. Yuri Abovyan, director of the Division of Strategic Use of Natural Resources of the Armenian Ministry of Ecology, concluded that "if there is no Sevan, there will be no drinking water, no Armenia."[28]

THE RIVERS OF THE COUNTRY

From a medical point of view, the rivers of the FSU, including the Don, the Volga, the Northern Dvina, the Ob, the Yenisey, and most others are actually hazardous to the health of the populations along their banks. River water has in recent decades become a source of outbreaks of typhoid fever, dysentery, cholera, viral hepatitis, toxic and chemical poisonings.[29] In mid-1993 medical authorities interviewed by a government newspaper cited salts of heavy metals, phenols, pesticides, and pathogenic bacteria and viruses found in the waters of the country to be the result of widespread dumping and general indifference to water regulations by organizations and individuals. Any long-term solution will have to include massive public education and far more vigorous enforcement of environmental regulations.[30]

CHAPTER 5

CHEMICAL AND BIOLOGICAL WARFARE
CENTERS AND OTHER SECRET FACILITIES

The Soviet Union's chemical and biological warfare efforts have been one of the country's best-hidden secrets. Now they may be the most frightening legacy of the cold war.

Even though the Soviet government's activities in this sphere were most carefully guarded, new revelations have confirmed previous suspicions of secret chemical and biological research and development. Much of the activity has been extensively described by James Adams in *The New Spies: Exploring the Frontiers of Espionage*. The first significant Western breakthrough in knowledge about Soviet research occurred in late 1988, when Dr. Vladimir Pasechnik, a senior official in the Ministry of Defense and a manager of one of the Soviet secret biotechnology laboratories near St. Petersburg, contacted a British MI6 official in Paris and defected to the United Kingdom. In extensive debriefings with British intelligence, Pasechnik subsequently described a vast network of secret facilities in the Biopreparat system, including his laboratory in St. Petersburg, two laboratories in Moscow, two more just outside Moscow, and one in Novosibirsk. Each of these produced deadly germ warfare agents. Five manufacturing plants employing 15,000 people operated in other parts of the country.[1]

According to Pasechnik, his laboratory—along with the Research Institute of Applied Microbiology at Obelinsk—developed a "super-plague," a new strain of tularemia, in 1983. Tularemia (discovered in Tulare, California) is a serious, infectious bacterial disease carried by direct human contact or through an insect bite. The same Soviet scientists were set to work on a new pneumonic plague two years later.[2] The defection in 1992 of another Russian scientist confirmed Pasechnik's information and revealed that research and development in biological weapons continued despite official governmental protestations to the contrary. The information from both sources convinced the intelligence community and senior officials on both sides of the Atlantic of the seriousness of Russian germ warfare efforts. This led to high-level objections from the Bush and Clinton administrations as well as from the British government.[3]

The initial reaction of both the Gorbachev and Yeltsin governments to Western accusations was to deny the existence of germ and chemical warfare activity. However, in February 1992 at Camp David, Boris Yeltsin admitted for the first time that there had been a secret chemical and biological warfare effort and stated that he had ordered it shut down. He repeated these assurances to President Clinton at the Vancouver summit in 1993.

Almost from the beginning there have been questions as to whether the Russian military has abided by the promises made by President Yeltsin to Presidents Bush and Clinton. These questions were raised anew in the autumn of 1993 when yet a third defector from the Biopreparat project revealed that germ warfare research was continuing secretly at various Russian research facilities and that a new facility was even being built at Lakhta near St. Petersburg. Work was reportedly continuing in defiance of Yeltsin's orders.[4]

In September 1992, Dr. Vil Mirzayanov, a Russian chemist, published statements in the Russian press and also provided information to the *Baltimore Sun* that Russia was developing and testing a new binary chemical weapon. This activity was contrary to promises made by Yeltsin to President Bush. The same scientist claimed that Russia currently possesses a chemical weapons stockpile of 60,000 to 70,000 tons, which would indicate a failure to live up to its promise to the United States to destroy 40,000 tons.[5] On January 27, 1994, Mirzayanov was detained for divulging state secrets connected with the development of secret weapons; he was released on February 22. The charges were dropped in April 1994 in the middle of his trial.

On April 7, 1994, President Yeltsin fired the former army general who headed Russia's chemical and biological disarmament program, Anatoliy Kuntsevich, for "numerous and gross violations" of his duties.[6]

It is still too early to determine whether the Russian government will now actually move to carry out its public pledges on chemical and biological warfare. In July 1994 it was estimated that the cost of destroying Russia's chemical weapons would be hundreds of millions of dollars. Further, Russian investigative journalists contended that the 1994 State Defense Order had not provided financing towards chemical weapons destruction.[7] Questions remain about the actual extent of the weapons stockpile, locations, and the activities of various secret chemical facilities. For example, in February 1994 it was reported that 690 tons of mustard gas, 225 tons of lewisite, and 210 tons of other unspecified chemical compounds were being stored at the village of Gornyy not far from the Volga.[8] The chemical weapons apparently had been stored there for considerable time in metal barrels and railroad tankers and now pose a danger to the population. New chemical "secret cities," facilities, and storage areas are constantly being pointed out. (Appendix A contains the most extensive list of these facilities found to date.)

VOZROZHDENIYE BIOLOGICAL WARFARE CENTER

The Biological Warfare Center on Vozrozhdeniye Island, in the shrinking Aral Sea, needs special attention because of the danger it poses. If the withdrawal of the sea continues as projected by Uzbek scientists, the formerly secret warfare laboratory may be connected by land to the surrounding areas by the year 2000, thus making dissemination of any lingering threats to health from the research activities conducted there easier. If past practices held, a thorough cleanup of the facility very likely was not performed before its closure. Work at Vozrozhdeniye island very likely led to disasters among the animal populations of the region. Careless operation of such facilities may have led to a massive fish die-off in 1976. In May 1988 about 500,000 antelope perished on the Turgay Steppe. In July 1989 an outbreak of animal plague occurred, in which flocks of sheep lost their wool and died.[9] Characteristically for a putative military-linked source of these problems, not one of the events were seriously investigated. International concern about the Vozrozhdeniye Center was initiated by Sweden in Geneva many years ago. This concern must be resurrected and carried beyond words to an actual investigation of the Center's potential harm to Russia as well as surrounding countries.

OTHER SECRET FACILITIES

The Vozrozhdeniye Island Biological Warfare Center is only one of numerous secret chemical, biological, and nuclear facilities where outside access has been extremely limited—even for Russian civilian officials. Many environmentalists and some officials believe that these plants present a special environmental threat. Russian environmentalists point to pollution indices and deterioration of the general health at these secret cities as evidence of the dangerous accidents and toxic dumping that are a deadly by-product of these facilities. It was only in May 1992 that the first serious public discussion of secret nuclear cities occurred. Viktor Mikhaylov, the minister of atomic industry, spoke at a meeting in Stavanger, Norway, about the existence of this network.

Prior to Mikhaylov's disclosures, the West knew little about the ten cities (a fictitious number) that were nominally members of the Atomgrad ("Atomic City") network, and nothing about the chemical and biological weapons facilities. The Atomic City network, established by Lavrenty Beria under Stalin's order to develop the atomic bomb, consisted of cities that were not shown on maps of the country, whose populations were not included in the Soviet censuses and not counted among published statistics on the research, development, testing and evaluation (RDT&E) workforce. Extraordinary efforts were undertaken to maintain the highest secrecy about their activities.

Varying estimates of the actual number of such secret cities— including those dedicated to military-related chemical and biological warfare activities—ranged from sixteen to eighty-seven. It is now possible from open sources to document at least thirty-eight such cities. (Appendix B provides the information currently available.) There may be additional small towns or settlements that may also be considered "closed," if not secret cities. If so, the total number could be in the hundreds, or even higher, according to anonymous well-informed sources; one indicated that there were eight hundred such places.

These nuclear, chemical and biological facilities are not only threatening to the world but are themselves perhaps under threat. The government now admits that the Atomgrad network, if not the others, is a target of mafia activity.[10] Dangerous material and trained personnel represent a potential illegal export commodity attractive to any regime or militant organization seeking to develop advanced weaponry for terror.

CHAPTER 6

POLLUTION OF THE AIR AND LAND

One institute of the Russian Academy of Medical Sciences has calculated that only 15 percent of the urban population of Russia lives in areas with "ecologically acceptable levels of pollution."[1] A Russian government resolution of March 16, 1990, identified forty-three cities in Russia as requiring urgent measures to reduce air pollution.[2] The former Russian Federation minister of health, Dr. A. I. Potapov, asserted separately that "to live longer, [one must] breathe less."

Atmospheric pollution, according to the 1992 *State Report on the Environment*, is now estimated to be responsible for 20 to 30 percent of the overall illness rate of the population. Forty percent more individuals are reported to be sick in the cities of Magnitogorsk, Novokuznetsk, Nizhniy Tagil, and Lipetsk—all centers of ferrous metallurgy—than in relatively nonpolluted cities.[3] High rates of bronchial asthma and skin allergies are blamed on petrochemical and organic synthetic materials produced in Sterlitamak, Ufa, and Chaykovskiy. In the city of Sterlitamak the oncological disease rate is twice as high as in nonindustrial urban areas, the stillbirth rate is six to seven times higher, the occurrence and development of congenital defects is three times higher, and the disease rate for bronchial asthma is six times higher.[4] The biotechnology industry in Svetloyarsk, Manurovo, and Shebekino is directly linked to the overall incidence of illness and to allergies in these locations. In the past ten years, birth defects in Russia overall have increased five times, but in Ufa seven times and in Salavat nine times. Congenital anomalies are tenfold higher than in the United States.[5]

TOXIC WASTE DUMPING, INDUSTRIAL AND TRANSPORT ACCIDENTS, AND CHEMICAL RESIDUES

In the 1980s, approximately one-third of all the world's industrial mishaps took place on the territory of the former Soviet Union.[6] In fact, on average, two serious pipeline accidents occur every day in Russia; one serious transportation accident each week; and one serious industrial accident per month.[7] Industrial and transportation accidents, breaks in pipelines, and intentional toxic dumping are among the main causes of pollution throughout the entire FSU.

TOXIC DUMPING

Deliberate dumping is the principal villain. Evidence shows that heavy metal toxic waste sites and "ordinary" toxic industrial waste dumping have spread throughout the urban setting. Currently some 106 billion tons of toxic waste are simply stacked in depots throughout Russia in conditions that threaten rivers and surroundings with contamination.[8]

Metallurgical plants alone, according to the Socio-Ecological Union's *Bulletin*, contaminate adjacent surface land with "280,000 tons of arsenic, more than 150,000 tons of copper, 120,000 tons of zinc, 90,000 tons of lead, 12,000 tons of nickel, and many others." These figures do not include poisoning of the surface land from cadmium, mercury, beryllium, and thallium.[9] Nor do they include the release of metals into the atmosphere (see Appendix F).

The former Ukrainian minister of environment, Dr. Yuri Shcherbak, told Senators Bill Bradley and John Kerry and Congressman James Leach, while they were on a trip in the region, that the area between Mariupol and Dnepropetrovsk in Ukraine is a "valley of death."[10] One hundred and two million tons of "highly toxic waste" is produced each year in Ukraine, plus another 22 billion tons of various uncategorized forms of waste.[11] Similar conditions have been reported in Ukraine and Russia as well as the other republics of the FSU. Industrial pollution is believed by all official accounts to be producing comparable conditions in many areas of the remainder of the FSU.

As noted, industrial accidents are another major contributor. In 1992, there were eighty-two accidents at chemical enterprises "involving destruction of production facilities and release of sizable volumes of toxic substances into the environment." According to a study commissioned by the Russian government, "On the whole, each year around 1,500 accidents associated with leakage of explosive and toxic products from production systems, fires, explosions and discharges of contaminated water into water basins occur in the chemical sectors of industry."[12] Major disasters have been reported at chemical enterprises in Ufa, Sterlitamak, Tomsk, Angarsk, Salavat, Stavropol, and other cities.[13] Located at these and other cities (such as Usol'ye-Sibirskoye, Kemerovo, and Dzerzhinsk) are large quantities of toxic and highly toxic materials used in production. There are "100 billion lethal human doses of chlorine and 100 billion lethal doses of ammonia and prussic acid" at these enterprises.[14] The study indicates that accidents with such materials occur frequently. Many of these plants are in the same cities revealed by Dr. Lev Fyedorov, a former senior researcher in the chemical warfare industry, as places where there are chemical weapon production facilities.[15]

PIPELINE AND TRANSPORTATION ACCIDENTS

An average of two major oil and gas pipeline spills occur every day, every year.[16] With oil and gas pipelines stretching over a network of 550,000 kilometers (about 340,000 miles), minor spills can add up to significant losses as well. Losses may account for up to 7 percent of the total annual Russian output; some reports put losses as high as 20 percent. Information provided to a reporter for *Nezavisimaya gazeta* by the Academy of Sciences indicates that 10 percent of these pipelines have been in use for more than thirty-five years. According to the Academy, twenty-five years is considered to be the operational life of such pipelines. Approximately 28,000 ruptures in the pipelines were recorded in 1991 alone.[17]

In a study report from by the Russian Federation President's Council for Ecological Policy in the spring of 1993, pipeline accidents were only one of several types of serious accidents discussed.[18] Transport of hazardous cargo was also hampered by "1,032 accidents and incidents" on Russian railroads. At the conference the principal concern was accidents involving the shipping of chlorine. Every year, 500,000 tons of chlorine are shipped in railroad tank cars, and about 90,000 tons are shipped in bottles and containers by motor and rail transport. Chlorine has been described as "the sole disinfectant used on a major scale to treat drinking water and liquid wastes," as well as an important raw material for many industrial sectors. The likelihood of an accident with chlorine was enhanced by the average distance of transport—around 1,500 kilometers (900 miles), with much being shipped over 4,500 kilometers (2,800 miles). With the current lack of infrastructure maintenance, the potential for contamination remains very high.[19]

There are 1,926 enterprises and organizations located in 448 cities and "other populated places" in Russia that continue to produce or use "highly active poisonous substances."[20] According to a professor at the Moscow Academy of Transport, and a senior researcher at the Russian Academy of Sciences, "conditions are likely only to worsen over the course of the next decade." Both believe that about 80 percent of all industrial enterprises in Russia would go bankrupt if forced to comply with environmental laws. "Russian politicians, who are all engaged in fierce internal battles, cannot afford to allow the bankruptcy of these enterprises because that would result in massive unemployment." As a result, reports of local officials being bribed to permit toxic dumping have been widespread.[21]

Air pollution emanating from flaring oil and gas at wellheads contributes to the total amount of poisonous substances. This also has major economic consequences, not only in terms of income forgone, but also in terms of the amount of funds available to clean up the environment. Given that perhaps half of the hard currency earnings of the former Soviet Union (principally from Russia) was derived from sales of oil to the West, it is completely incomprehensible that more than 10 billion cubic meters were flared off in Russia and not recovered in 1991; in 1992, 15 billion cubic meters were flared.

Nine unspecified regions are particularly subject to chemical dangers according to Vladimir P. Vorfolomeyev. The potential for accidents at hydroelectric installations endangers the populations of twenty-two oblasts, *krays*, and autonomous republics, as well as 2,713 cities and villages. Approximately 36 million people reside in forty-eight cities where they were exposed to PDKs for highly toxic substances that were ten times higher than the allowable standard.[22]

DIOXIN

In Russia the most serious environmental threat may be from dioxin, a chlorinated hydrocarbon insecticide widely employed in the FSU and a highly toxic by-product in the manufacture of chemicals. It is a carcinogen that causes damage to the reproductive, endocrine, and immune systems in birds, fish, and mammals, including human beings. It is now considered so toxic that it is no longer manufactured for household use in the United States.

The leadership of the Soviet Union reached a judgment that dioxin was "the most serious threat" to the country in early 1990, although the government made every effort to keep this fact from the general public. While Mikhail Gorbachev was still in power, the heads of the KGB, the State Planning Committee, and the Academy of Sciences admitted that dioxin was so widespread throughout the land, air, and water that it posed the maximum risk to the country.[23]

In the 1992 *State Report on the Environment,* dioxin pollution was considered to be "a genuine threat" in several Russian cities, in the zones of intensive rice farming in the Kuban, the lower Volga, the Far East, and the Sea of Azov regions. Concentration of polychlorinated dibenzodioxins (PCDDs) and dibenzofurans (PCDFs) in the surface water of several Russian cities exceeded the safety limits by 1.2 to 10.5 times. In Ufa, dioxin concentrations in the soil exceeded the presumed safe level of exposure by 160 times and in Chapayevsk up to 75 times, although in some areas of Chapayevsk the soil concentration was in excess of 2,000 times the limit and the air content 7 times. In all of Bashkortostan (formerly called Bashkiriya), including Ufa, *Izvestiya* reports that "an infant gets seventy percent of the maximum allowable dioxin with a liter of its mother's breast milk."[24] In the United States, by contrast, an Environmental Protection Agency (EPA) study indicated that "four to twelve percent of the amount of dioxin that a person receives in a lifetime could come from breastfeeding during the first year of life."[25]

PESTICIDES AND FERTILIZERS

For a long time there have been widespread reports that pesticides and fertilizers have been used in excessive quantities and stored in improper and dangerous ways. Since the collapse of the Soviet Union public agencies charged with controlling the use of pesticides and fertilizers have become less effective both for budgetary reasons and because of a general breakdown of governmental authority.

According to official statistics, 52 percent of agricultural storage facilities in Russia do not meet environmental protection requirements.[26] In a majority of these cases, chemicals are stored virtually out in the open.[27] In 1992 alone there were 994 cases in which bodies of water were poisoned.[28] The Russian Federation Committee on Fishing reported massive fish kills in the watersheds of the Volga River and the Sea of Azov. Two million fish—pike, roach, perch, carp, and silver carp—died in the Merchetka River in 1992 as a result of pesticide runoffs.[29] In the same year, 84,000 fish died in the Anna River, which flows into the Cheboksary Reservoir, as a result of pesticide runoff from hops cultivation along the river.[30] The "Green World" (*Zelenyy Svit*) association has asked the general prosecutor of Ukraine to investigate the illegal import of hundreds of tons of pesticides from countries where such pesticides are banned from use.[31] In Russia approximately 100,000 tons of unusable pesticides have reportedly accumulated at the Ministry of Agriculture and Foodstuffs' warehouses alone.

According to the United Nations Environment Programme (UNEP), "at least 40,000 people worldwide are killed each year by the misuse of pesticides, and up to 1 million are made ill or permanently damaged."[32] There is no comparable figure available for the FSU; however, statistics on child morbidity as a result of exposure to chemicals while working in the cotton fields in Central Asia suggest that illness and even death from misuse of fertilizers may be widespread. In Uzbekistan in 1987, 123 schoolchildren had to be taken to the hospital suffering from poisoning. Apparently, nitrogen fertilizer had been stored in the open air, unprotected from rain. The fertilizer filtered through the soil to the wells, which were not tested by local officials. It is almost impossible these days to pick up any local newspaper in the former Soviet Union and not read of a similar incident of contaminated land or water.

Heptyl

An additional threat to a healthy ecological system is posed by heptyl, a liquid fuel used in nearly all Soviet nuclear missiles, which has already resulted in heavy contamination of the Plesetsk missile range in Arkhangel'sk oblast (and undoubtedly various seas in the far north). Heptyl is a "highly toxic neuroparalytic, carcinogenic, and asphyxiating substance" with a maximum permissible concentration in air of only 0.00001 milligrams per cubic meter.[33]

Heptyl is highly volatile. It oxidizes when exposed to the air, forming a number of chemical compounds that are even more dangerous than the original substance.[34] The rockets that fire heptyl fuel create toxic exhaust gases during ignition. An additional danger is created with the release of the first rocket stage, containing approximately 700 kg of unused fuel in the engine, tanks, and hoses. The danger to personnel handling the material as well as to nearby communities is extreme.

According to a report in *Rossiyskye vesti*, when the Plesetsk test site in northern Russia was in use more than eight million hectares

(17.4 million acres, an area of land roughly 150 by 200 miles) was "heavily contaminated" by rockets using heptyl for fuel.[35] The local authorities at Plesetsk Cosmodrome were actually sued in 1994 by the Arkhangel'sk Oblast Environmental Protection Committee for 1.2 billion rubles. While contesting the unprecedented claim against the military as excessive, the authorities were forced to admit that rocket launching had indeed caused damage to nature.[36]

In Kazakhstan alone, one member of parliament reported that on approximately 1.5 million hectares of land situated in a triangle between Ural'sk, Guriyev, and Astrakhan, "virtually everything has been destroyed by weapons testing from rockets and aircraft."[37]

Missile launch bases in Russia, Ukraine, Belarus, and Kazakhstan are all sites of potential heptyl problems. Fuel stored on the bases and contained in the missiles themselves could leak and oxidize, causing serious health hazards. Mobile missiles on either launch vehicles or rail cars may also contain heptyl at risk of accidental release. Naturally transportation of the fuel itself, either by rail or road, also poses a threat. One major railroad accident involving hazardous fuel occurred in Volgograd in 1992. The total number of locations where heptyl is stored is not known, but the number of fixed missile launch sites is more than twenty-four.[38] There may be up to 150,000 tons of the supertoxic substance throughout the FSU.[39] Recent proposals to chemically convert heptyl to fertilizer need to be carefully reviewed so that in the process no additional environmental hazards are created and the end product is safe for use.

CONSEQUENCES OF CHEMICAL CONTAMINATION

"YELLOW CHILDREN"

Dr. Vladimir Lupandin, a physician serving with an advisory group attached to Alexsey Yablokov's office and a member of the board of directors of the Socio-Ecological Union, has been studying the unusually high rate of "yellow children" among births in Altayskiy *kray*. Lupandin eliminated jaundice as a possible cause of this unusual illness. He is also certain that the phenomenon is not caused by radioactivity from past atomic weapons testing in nearby Semipalatinsk. Rather, his research results point toward toxicological causes—chemicals affecting the water and food products consumed in the area and, in particular, heptyl inadvertently consumed by the mother.

Writing in *Poisk*, the newspaper of the scientific community, Lupandin notes that this phenomenon, first reported in 1988–89, was marked not only by a "yellowing" of the skin but also by serious diseases of the blood—anemia and reduced numbers of thrombocytes (platelets) and normal erythrocytes (red blood cells)—and of the central nervous system. In the spring of 1988, ten of these "yellow children" died soon after birth in the Loktevskiy *rayon*. In October 1989, nearly 72 percent of sixty newborns in the Tal'menskiy *rayon* were "yellow children." In 1990, 28 percent of all newborns in the same district were seriously jaundiced and nearly three-quarters of these babies suffered from diseases of the central nervous system. "Yellow children" exhibiting similar characteristics shortly appeared in six other *rayons* of the Altayskiy *kray*.[40]

PROBLEMS WITH FOOD

Shortages and lack of variety continually plagued the Soviet Union and still persist today. Much of the available food either is not fit for consumption or tends to produce detrimental health effects. Throughout the FSU there have been numerous reports of salmonella, dysentery, and other diseases caused by contaminated food. Food contamination has most likely increased as a result of the disarray in the economy and society and the failure of the government to enforce health regulations. Only in the past year has Moscow attempted to protect the population from what they eat.

Yablokov estimated that 30 percent of all food was contaminated in 1990, with 10 percent actually toxic to the consumer. Approximately 40 percent of all baby food is contaminated with pesticides, herbicides, and especially nitrates. These undoubtedly contribute to the growing number of digestive illnesses and other maladies associated with consumption of poor-quality foods. Paradoxically, these trends are mitigated to some degree by farmers' increasing inability to afford the inflated costs of nitrates, pesticides, and herbicides; as a consequence, most are applying them less frequently.

MANAGEMENT OF THE LAND

Details recently made available on the extent of wind and water erosion, salination, swamping, waterlogging, compacting of the earth, and loss of humus demonstrate that such problems abound throughout the FSU. Approximately 50 percent of all arable land needs remediation and better management. Significant increases in agricultural productivity will depend upon the successful treatment of soil ailments as well as effective privatization of the farm sector.[41]

Desertification in the Kalmykia region of southern Russia and in the Aral Sea region has contributed to the reduction of arable land available. Deserts are expanding in Kalmykia at a rate of 30,000 acres per year, adding to the 400,000 to 500,000 acres of Europe's only desert. The desiccation of the Aral Sea is leading to an expansion of the Kyzyl-kum desert. Polluted water, diverted (for cotton irrigation) from the Aral Sea's feeder rivers, leaks into the subsoil from unlined canals. This effectively sterilizes the soil by leaving poisonous mineral and salt deposits, thereby adding to the desertification of the region.

RUSSIA'S RED BOOK: PARKS, PRESERVES, AND NATURAL SANCTUARIES

As a consequence of pollution, poor land management practices, soil erosion, salination, desertification, and the other destructive environmental changes, increasing varieties of vegetation and wildlife—603 to date—are now listed in the Russian "Red Book" of endangered species. The *State Report on the State of the Environment of the Russian Federation in 1992* included data from an earlier edition of the Red Book that listed 562 plant species and 246 animal species as endangered in Russia alone.[42] In 1991 an estimated $1 billion of contraband trade in rare and endangered animals and plants took place, with some two-thirds of the business emanating from the former USSR.[43] If anything, the rate of trade in the FSU has increased since then.

The governmental agencies charged with the task of enforcing environmental protection regulations are seriously underfunded and overstretched. In some cases, local agency officials are the worst offenders, having discovered that their positions can be very lucrative in this era of change. By taking bribes, ignoring illegal dumping of hazardous materials, permitting overcutting of trees, and allowing the poaching of protected species, many have gone from being low-paid officials to rich "entrepreneurs."[44]

Early in 1993 two leading figures spoke before the Russian Academy of Sciences regarding the ongoing illegal pursuit of rare animals. Vladimir Sokolov, a leading biologist and member of the Academy of Medical Sciences, asserted that "there is literally not a single species of beneficial animal protected by 'The Red Book' that is not threatened by . . . mercenary lawlessness."[45] Gennady Galkin, procurator of the Russian Federation Department of Oversight for the Fulfillment of Environmental Legislation, spoke on the seizure of land from protected parks, forest areas, and nature preserves. He noted that increasing numbers of geologists, loggers, and other citizens are infringing on the conservation of these areas. Illegal hunting has taken place throughout the entire Federation. Corruption among the nature conservation agency staff is so rampant that the guardians themselves need to be guarded. In Galkin's opinion, "the natural world is in jeopardy."[46]

THREAT TO THE FORESTS

After the Brazilian rain forests, the immense Russian forests provide the world's largest natural reservoir for absorption of carbon dioxide and production of oxygen. One Russian environmental expert estimated that the total carbon content of Russian forests is actually higher than that of the Amazon basin rain forests. The significance of the Russian forests for global climate is tremendous.

Officially Russia loses 5 million acres of the Siberian forest each year from fire, pollution, and overcutting—almost as much as the losses in the rain forest of Brazil (around 7 million acres). Reforestation officially is recorded as covering 3.7 million acres annually. However, supplementary information from satellite observations provided by Grigoriy S. Golitsyn's report on forest lands indicates that official data understate the losses to the forests by 200 to 300 percent.[47] Yablokov's unofficial figure of 35 million acres lost annually is six times the official figure. If these numbers are correct, the denuding of the Siberian forests has the potential to contribute more to global climate change than the assault on the Amazon basin.

Chemical pollution of the air and acid rain also have reduced the forest area by almost 1.5 million acres and have threatened an additional 2.5 million acres, according to official estimates, since the early 1970s. In a forest zone near the heavily polluting Noril'sk nickel combine, 740,000 acres have died; near the Bratsk aluminum plant, 345,000 acres; around Irkutsk, 170,000 acres; near the Severonikel' plant on the Kola Peninsula, 270,000 acres. These tremendous losses certainly will lead to future shortages in forest resources and may cause other problems such as wind and water erosion.

The forests are suffering because of improper forest management, extensive and frequent fires, clear-cutting, and political crises. The Armenian-Azerbaijan conflict with its disruption of energy supplies has led townsfolk to chop down trees for fuel. Excessive clear-cutting and other poor management practices continue to account for a 40 percent loss from the amount of timber harvested, four times more waste than in other developed countries.[48] Uncollected timber from Russian forests at one point floated into Norwegian waters in such large amounts that the Norwegians were able to harvest large quantities from massive rafts of logs.

A major influence in the overcutting of Russian forests over the last several years has been the government's overriding interest in obtaining hard currency. This has produced agreements with foreign, particularly South Korean, companies for the sale of timber. Through these deals, some areas of the Siberian forest have become overexploited. Fortunately, thanks to protests by Russian environmental groups, this practice was halted in the spring of 1994. Nonetheless, irretrievable losses have already occurred.

CHAPTER 7

TOWARD A
WESTERN ECOLOGICAL AGENDA

The Communist party and Soviet government created the current ecological and health crisis over a period of seventy-four years. It will take a good amount of time for the successor governments to stop fully the momentum and to reverse the ongoing destruction of the air, land, and water. Available estimates predict that the corrective processes will take decades to achieve and will consume unprecedented, perhaps unattainable, amounts of monetary and physical resources. As a result, the mere process of thinking about the task becomes a daunting, numbing psychological experience.

"Everything is going wrong," a Russian friend told the author recently, "everything needs repair; every problem is connected to some other problem. We don't know where to begin and we have no money." A senior U. S. Agency for International Development (AID) official put the dilemma in similar terms after the author's recent State Department briefing on the ecological and health problems facing the FSU: "Your data are compelling; my problem is how to do all the tasks needed with the limited funds available."[1]

Western governments, seeking an overall health and environmental strategy for the East, face a major policy dilemma of competing demands for scarce resources. However, it is not only a simple issue of insufficient money to go around. Rather, the real problem stems from a debate over priorities, particularly within the Western foreign assistance community, where institutional positions are often deeply entrenched. This debate has resulted in a fundamental conflict of developmental philosophies: What is the principal goal of our assistance—humanitarian relief or nation building, or perhaps both, with the former a short-term goal and the latter setting a long time horizon?

For example, major sources of the health crisis within the FSU today are industrial and agricultural pollution. In response, should Western aid therefore be focused on the immediate humanitarian needs of the afflicted population or on the structural causes of poor health, namely, resource allocation and industrial and agricultural policy? How deeply can any Western government afford to become engaged in the massive effort to reform and reconstruct the economies of the FSU? What is really possible for any one or a combination of Western governments to undertake given the resources at their disposal? Should demonstration projects be given priority or should regional ecosystems be attacked as a whole?

These are not abstract questions. There has recently been a palpable increase in anti-Americanism throughout the FSU, derived from a widely shared perception that, at a time of need, promised Western assistance has not been delivered. The real living standards for the vast majority of citizens of the FSU declined markedly over the past three years. Western "experts" have visited time and time again, asked the same questions over and over, have lectured and gone away, leaving behind little that is visible or meaningful to the average citizen. The prospect of International Monetary Fund (IMF) loans means nothing when the common person cannot even afford basic foodstuffs or medicine. Recent anecdotal evidence suggests that some Russians, at least, view the economic situation as improving over the last year, though this is difficult to verify quantitatively. However, for pensioners and those on fixed salaries, the situation remains grim.

The United States is not the only, nor even the worst, offender in terms of appearing to promise much and deliver little; it has become, however, the most frequent target of criticism largely because of its leadership role. Many Russians suspect Washington's motives; some wonder if it is destroying their economy through a combination of bad advice and neglect, or if the proffered assistance is just a device to sell American-made products and services while at the same time eliminating their Russian equivalents. This type of complaint is heard particularly from the Russian nuclear industry.

Complicating any search for an appropriate Western aid strategy is the question of finding the right mix of economic and ecological goals. Fundamental to any satisfactory policy formula is the charting of a course of sustainable economic development. Yet, the conundrum is that economic growth is rarely achieved without some environmental cost; conversely, desirable ecological solutions generally translate into a short-run economic debit. In a growing economy, the economic/ecological trade-offs are difficult but usually manageable over the long term although they sometimes cause considerable pain to a particular sector of the economy or segment of the society. In the case of the FSU, massive damage has already been inflicted on the environment, while the economy has been thrown into a tailspin (an official production decline of 20 percent over a single year); in these circumstances the trade-offs are hard to identify and even harder to defend politically.[2]

For the Russian government, for example, the polluting factory presents a difficult dilemma: Should the government maintain the factory, knowing that its operation could create health problems over the long term, or should it close the factory, accepting the immediate and direct cost of losing an enterprise that is possibly (considering the absence of a general government safety net) the sole source for employment, health services, housing, and other social support for the local population? Can that factory be closed for any reason if it is the lone producer of a good—as is too often the case in the Soviet industrial system, with its penchant for large, monopolistic enterprises—that is essential for the continued operation of a number of other firms?

Frederick Kempe, in his book *Siberian Odyssey*, relates a story of a local council that had voted to shut down the Kemerovo Coking and Chemical Plant, the largest employer and taxpayer in Kemerovo, because of large emissions of sulfur pollution. The plant's director, a lifelong communist, made a deal with the city that he would help it with food and medical supplies if the council would stay the factory's execution. "If you think too much about ecology, you won't have food to eat," the plant director later told Kempe.[3] Sentiments such as this are rampant throughout the FSU.

The danger for the West is policy paralysis. Unable to sort out priorities when there is never enough money available, Western governments may end up doing too little, too late or, maybe even worse, adopting prematurely a scattergun package of small, unrelated, "feel-good" assistance programs that neither engage the real problem nor produce any permanent solution.

There needs to be a new way of thinking about the problem. First, it is essential to stop thinking that environmental objectives need to be sacrificed on the altar of economic growth. This has been the principal error of the World Bank, as its president Lewis T. Preston admitted in mid-1994: "The mistake the Bank has paid the highest price for is not recognizing the importance of the environment."[4] The apparent decision of the Bank to give Russia $110 million ($45 million of which would be grant aid) to implement a series of nature conservation projects represents an important step towards establishing new, environmentally sensitive priorities.[5]

Second, there should be recognition that not everything can or should be solved at once. The proper Western response requires an understanding that the intertwined environmental and economic tasks faced by the FSU can be separated into a short-term and a long-term agenda. The immediate tasks are as much political as they are humanitarian: The ex-Soviet states need the kind of Western aid programs that will reach the average citizen and will build institutional and citizen blocs within the body politic in support of environmentally sensitive policies.

The structural problems of reshaping the economy and eliminating the worst sources of pollution will take decades, cost billions of dollars, and require an internationally coordinated attack. For now the immediate objective is to organize for the job. What is needed is an international mechanism for reaching common decisions and coordinating efforts for a comprehensive attack on the problems.

TASK ONE: PREPARE FOR THE LONG HAUL

The extent and depth of the ecological damage and health problems currently facing the FSU argue strongly in favor of a comprehensive and coherent multinational and multiyear approach. The governments of the FSU face a dangerous future: production is falling, public revenues are in decline, and there is increased demand for subsidies as a matter of social and political survival. The socialist command economy has not quite been abandoned; a new market economy is not yet fully in place. Caught between the old system, which failed, and a new vision of the future that they do not quite know how to implement, the Russian and other governments of the former Soviet Union are finding it very difficult to implement hard decisions on economic policy, let alone deal with their major environmental and health problems.

Emergency humanitarian assistance represents at best a palliative. It buys time and it may protect governments, for a time, from the anger of their citizenry. However, in the absence of any signs of an improved economic future, the political direction of any of the states of the FSU is unpredictable.

Since the breakup of the Soviet Union, the United States has considered the transformation of the successor countries into democratic governments to be in its national security interest, and has used political openness and stability as the chief criterion in providing aid. While this is still a worthy strategy, it is no longer the only national security issue to be considered. Today the United States must also base its aid packages on environmental problems as an important facet of national security. To date our efforts to aid Russia and the other states have been remarkably uncertain and uncoordinated. The problem is not simply the level of total Western assistance pledged, it is the slowness with which such aid has been implemented, the duplication of efforts, and the absence of any overall strategy or set of priorities that is most worrisome. At times, in the conduct of efforts to help the FSU, Western governments appear as if novices in providing foreign assistance.

Toward a Western Environmental Strategy

If the most important Western objective in the former Soviet Union is support of democracy, and the second is to help in the transition to a free market economy, the third surely must be the protection of the environment. Building ecological and health considerations into long-term aid strategies makes sense in at least three ways: First, it recognizes the reality that economics and environmental protection are necessarily interrelated. Any effort to restructure and rebuild the old, inefficient, and polluting Soviet industrial complex and agriculture could have both beneficial and potentially harmful effects on the environment. The West's challenge is to encourage the governments of the FSU to get it right. If the United States does nothing else, it should at minimum be looking at its assistance and investment policies to ensure that it is not adding to pollution problems. We need, for example, to focus our aid and investment in the petroleum field in the areas of preventing unnecessary losses through pipeline accidents and the flaring of natural gas, rather than solely on new production.

Second, it concentrates Western assistance in those areas that are best understood, and therefore most accepted by the target populations. Western initiatives are increasingly viewed with great suspicion by a large part of the population, perceived as aimed only at dismantling the old Soviet economy or giving foreign investors a leg up. The "market economy" is still widely associated with illegal "black market" operations, profiteering by the local mafia, and a radical and still unproved economic theory. On the other hand, Western assistance and investment aimed at reducing waste or cleaning up the air, water, or land is still welcomed by the populace.

Third, application of environmental and humanitarian criteria provides the Western policymaker with an analytical tool for sorting through desired programs to determine which ones best serve the global interest.

First Steps: The Indonesian Model. The most pressing need for Western governments is to develop a single mechanism for coordinating aid strategies over the long term. What is required is a set of institutions that will engage the governments of the former Soviet Union, Western donor countries, key international financial institutions (IFIs), and private organizations in an annual process of reviewing project performance to date, establishing (or reestablishing) future priorities, and pledging the next cycle of financial assistance.

This will not be a new experience for Western governments, they do not need to reinvent the wheel. In a number of major Western efforts since World War II, beginning with the launching of the Marshall Plan in Europe, a number of creative mechanisms have been developed for coordinating economic development policy and assistance programs. Probably the simplest, and the closest parallel to the FSU today, is the aid mechanism created for Indonesia in the late 1960s, through the establishment of the Inter-governmental Group for Indonesia (IGGI).

The political impetus for the creation of the IGGI grew out of the special circumstances in which Indonesia found itself at the end of the 1960s. The United States and its Western allies were seeking a way to provide aid to the new Suharto government, after the fall of the country's leader from independence, Sukarno, while avoiding the possibility that much of that assistance might be repaid to the Soviet Union for debts undertaken by Sukarno.

Two conditions present in Indonesia in the 1960s were analogous to those that confront the West today with regard to the FSU. First, it was obvious that after years of socialist economic experimentation, Western efforts to advance the Indonesian economy were likely to take decades; and second, Western governments needed some mechanism to maximize their efforts in Indonesia through a coordinated assistance strategy.

Ultimately the solution that Western governments came up with was less an institution than an organized, ad hoc policy process. Each year, on a date previously agreed to, the Indonesian government, Western donor countries, the IFIs (IBRD, IMF, UNIDO, ADB, etc.) and nongovernmental advisory groups would meet to review the aid program and to pledge the next tranche of Western assistance. Approximately sixty to ninety days prior to this IGGI meeting, resident missions of the World Bank, the IMF, aid groups, and donor countries would issue their own annual reports, providing project reviews, program assessments, and estimates of future assistance requirements.[6]

The process was pragmatic and flexible in its implementation—there were very few rules or agreements, and it was understood that financial pledges by donor countries were nonbinding and subject to later governmental review and legislative approval—but it had the useful quality of forcing all parties to keep talking to each other, all the time. More important, the annual consultations fairly quickly translated into a program and planning process that approached Indonesian economic development over longer periods of time.

Coordinating Western Aid Strategy. How Western governments talk to each other is largely a reflection of style and politics. In the end governments will choose the mechanism with which they are most comfortable. There are a variety of organizations already in existence that can play a coordinating role with regard to Western assistance to the FSU; the two most obvious to come to mind are the OECD and the G-7. Another international institution of potential utility is the Global Environment Facility, established by the United Nations and the World Bank, to which the United States and other aid-giving countries have already pledged $2 billion over the next three years to help poor countries fulfill their Rio de Janeiro environmental conference commitments.[7]

However, any mechanism that has as its objective the coordination of Western aid efforts to the FSU will have to contain certain components: First, it must have the flexibility and nonbinding quality that permits donor countries, international organizations, and other parties to discuss future plans that are still subject to various modifications. Second, the governments of the FSU must feel that they play an integral role in the planning process. The aid strategy should be something that is coming out of Moscow, or Kiev, rather than being generated by bureaucrats in Washington or Tokyo. Third, the planning process, including both policy program review and future financial pledges, should be viewed as a continuous effort, updated each year or on an ad hoc basis in response to emergency situations.

SOME INITIAL PRIORITIES: THE YABLOKOV LIST

In March of 1994, Aleksey Yablokov said that the West needed to be concerned about three particular dangers to the global environment from Russia. He argued that these potential threats would probably appear so serious to Western states as to outweigh all other environmental problems in the FSU. First, there was a significant possibility of a second "Chernobyl-like" nuclear accident as devastating as what had already occurred in Ukraine. Second, he warned that past and future radioactive and chemical dumping could result in the "poisoning" of the Arctic, the Baltic, and other northern bodies of water. Third, he feared that the great Siberian forests of Russia, the world's second largest woodland area after the Brazilian rain forest, were being destroyed at a rate that could have a dangerous impact on global warming. Fortunately, there appears to be widespread consensus among the Nordic states, the Baltic littoral states, Western Europe, and Japan on the criticality of these problem areas. As the West begins to sort out its long-term foreign assistance agenda these three areas need to be addressed through a series of initiatives.

Preventing Future Chernobyls. As described earlier, there are sixteen reactors of the RBMK (Chernobyl) type and eleven first-generation VVER-type reactors, which are of primary concern to both Western and Russian officials. Between the years 2001 and 2009, the Russian government plans gradually to close down all nuclear power plants designed before 1973.[8]

Any plan to close these reactors more rapidly will require a major Western commitment to assist Russia, Ukraine, and Lithuania in developing alternative power sources. While reactors produce only 12 percent of Russian and 20 percent of Ukrainian total energy requirements, within specific geographic regions the energy dependence is much higher. Lithuania obtains 50 percent of its total energy from its nuclear power plant; while one report, without specifying further, referred to nuclear power providing up to two-thirds of energy requirements in "northern Russia."[9]

One solution would be to encourage the Russians to move rapidly toward efficient gas-turbine cogenerators, possibly by converting current jet engine production facilities to turbine production. The U.S. Department of Commerce, along with the Export-Import Bank and the Overseas Private Investment Corporation, should begin discussions on a priority basis with the Russian, Ukrainian, and Lithuanian governments with a view to putting together a package that would be attractive to U.S. corporate investors.

However, support for gas-turbine power generation should be balanced with a willingness of the United States, together with other nuclear-capable countries such as Sweden, France, Germany, and Japan, to work with appropriate energy ministries throughout the FSU to modernize and make safer the remaining nuclear reactors. Recent efforts by the Clinton administration to reduce or eliminate the liability of foreign corporations and governments in cases of accident should expedite this effort. The willingness to assist Russia in the nuclear field is particularly important because there is a long-standing and deeply imbedded suspicion in Russian nuclear circles that Western efforts to close down dangerous reactors reflects a conspiracy to "strangle the Russian's nuclear power industry."[10] Such people feel that any move to close down nuclear reactors could be irreversible. "Russia could lose all scientific, technical and industrial potential it has today in nuclear power," Valeriy Menshikov, then deputy chairman of the Supreme Soviet Committee on Ecology, wrote in 1993.[11]

Replacing the first-generation RBMK- and VVER-type power reactors will take years and cost many billions of dollars. Jonathan C. Brown, the World Bank's division chief for infrastructure, energy and environment, estimates a price tag of between $6 billion and $8 billion. Ivan Selin, chairman of the U.S. Nuclear Regulatory Commission, has judged that the cost may eventually climb to $20 billion. Private estimates run even higher. The European-based multinational engineering firm Asea Brown Boveri has sent engineers to inspect some of the Soviet plants in Eastern Europe, and the firm's executive vice president, Eberhard von Korber, has projected that it could cost $50 billion to rehabilitate, decommission, and replace dangerous plants in the ex-Soviet republics and could take five to ten years to shut off nuclear reactors that he believes "should be closed down at once."[12]

Nevertheless, it is in the West's interest to launch a program as soon as possible that moves the Russian government in a direction of replacing all the first-generation RBMK and VVER power reactors. A logical place to begin would be assisting the Ukrainian government in fulfilling its pledge to close the remaining two RBMK reactors at

Chernobyl as requested by G-7 experts.[13] According to Kiev radio, early in 1994 the European Union pledged to provide financial assistance to build two new reactors in Ukraine on the condition that Chernobyl is closed.[14] In June, however, the European Union seemed to change its collective mind, and it is now supporting retrofitting and "improvements" in the RBMK reactors. The twelve European Union countries agreed in July to supply up to $600 million for nuclear safety in Ukraine.[15]

Simultaneously, a major effort is needed to promote conservation of energy. Lighting at home or in institutions should be converted to low-power-draining lightbulbs, such as fluorescents. In addition, there should be a widespread replacement of electric motors installed thirty or more years ago. Substituting more efficient devices could reduce the demand for electric power derived from nuclear energy and from coal (which is not only inefficient but the source of carcinogenic substances when burned at improper temperature levels).

Unfortunately, conservation is a concept that is far from the cognizance of most plant managers, households, ministries, and institutions, especially the military. An effort to educate these groups could have positive results if carried out skillfully. Unfortunately, in an atmosphere of high inflation and harsh economic realities the last thing that factory managers want to discuss, let alone implement, is energy conservation. Thus, in this introductory period of conservation, a "polluter pays" approach in combination with user fees should be implemented. A low payment rate should set initially, with gradual increases to come at a later date. This approach should not so much aim at punishing the behavior as correcting it. A system that is too harsh at the beginning would draw too much income away from pension plans to invest in costly energy-saving devices and would add another tax that most factory managers cannot afford. However, whatever measures are imposed, they must be enforced. Russia can no longer continue the bad habit of passing, promulgating, and signing laws and regulations that never take effect.

A second high-priority project would be to assist the Russian government in implementing its proposed closure of the last plutonium-producing reactor at Krasnoyarsk. Additional U.S. support in subsequent years would be a matter for later discussion and negotiation between the two governments. If properly designed, a long-term U.S. program to replace antiquated nuclear generators with newer, safer ones would be a multibillion-dollar stimulus for U.S. industry and exports.

International Conferences to Save the Arctic Ocean and Baltic Sea.
The environmental threat should help define Western aid priorities. It
is urgent that leaders move to prevent further degradation of the two
bodies of water most threatened by chemical and radioactive dumping: the Arctic Ocean and Baltic Sea. The danger is already clearly
understood by Western Europeans and the Japanese; in many respects
the Europeans concerned about the Baltic and the Japanese disturbed
by conditions in the Arctic and Far Eastern waters are ahead of the
United States in monitoring the problem and pressing the Russian
government to take corrective action.

Scandinavians are extremely worried about their Russian neighbor, particularly regarding the situation on the Kola Peninsula
(Murmansk oblast), with its vast military forces, its nuclear reactors, its
nuclear waste dumps on land and in ship holds, as well as nonnucle-
ar industrial pollution sources. Because of their fears about the
"world's largest concentration of nuclear installations," Norway—as
agreed to by the other Scandinavians and the Murmansk oblast
authorities—has already installed the first of eight automatic radioactive monitoring stations. As a consequence, the atmospheric situation
in Murmansk oblast is known in Norway twenty-four hours a day.[16]
In addition, the Norwegians set aside 20 million Norwegian kroner
(about $2.6 million) for the modernization of the Russian nuclear elec-
tric power station on the Kola Peninsula at Polyarnyye Zori.[17]

Separately, the Finns have allocated 9 million markkas (about
$1.5 million) for modernization of the Polyarnyye Zori and Sosnovy
Bor (near St. Petersburg) stations. Of this money, 3.5 million markkas
is for improvements in the safety systems and operation of Polyarnyye
Zori; 4 million is for modernization of the Sosnovy Bor station's operating and servicing system, and 1 million for materials and equipment needed at both stations. Finland authorized 6.4 million markkas
the year before (1992) for inspection, planning, and determination
of priorities.

The Norwegians' sense of alarm was heightened when they wit-
nessed unusual activities at the Polyarnyye Zori station on March 5,
1994. Members of the Norwegian Parliament's Environment Committee watched a group of Russian technicians rush into the reactor room
in which they were present. The technicians immediately began to
screw down the top of one of the reactors. One month later the
Norwegians were told that there had been a leak of radioactive water.[18]
The Norwegian foreign minister, in appealing to public opinion at

home and in the rest of Europe about the threat emanating from this power station, which is admittedly far from the population centers of Europe, declared that Norway could not by itself tackle the enormous cleanup operation and that "an international mobilization is needed to solve the problems."

Early in 1993, Moscow agreed to a German offer to provide assistance without charge eliminating nuclear and chemical weapons as specified by treaty in Russia.[19] The Germans will also help build storage tanks for highly enriched uranium and plutonium from dismantled bombs and in stocks. Being so close to Russia, Germany clearly has an interest in reducing any threat from accidents or other uses of nuclear materials as soon as possible.

Japanese officials are so concerned about the potential danger from various forms of Russian dumping—particularly radioactive waste and heptyl fuel—that they have requested permission of the Russian government to send in teams of technicians and advisers to help in lessening the danger. It was strong condemnation by the Japanese populace, and the ensuing protests by the Japanese Foreign Ministry, in 1993 that caused the Russian government to delay further radioactive dumping in the Sea of Japan. The Japanese and Russians have created a Bilateral Commission on Nuclear Waste and have agreed in principle jointly to build a radioactive waste treatment plant in the Far East. The Japanese government also has agreed in the interim on the building of a mobile storage center for Russian radioactive waste in Japan.[20]

The Baltic states have moved well along in terms of developing a collective approach to the threats facing the Baltic Sea. The 1974 Baltic Sea Convention, expanded in 1992, has led to numerous efforts to clean up the region. For example, the Baltic Eco Association sponsors creative, small-scale projects aimed at reducing the industrial, agricultural, and military waste in the sea.[21] Although Baltic Eco Association experts estimate that more than 28 billion Swedish kroner (about $3.8 billion) over a period of twenty to thirty years would be required to restore the Baltic to its 1950s state, the assumption is that small and concrete efforts that are economically practicable and achievable in the short term can also make a significant difference.[22]

Little had been accomplished in terms of major cleanup programs under the Baltic Sea Convention by early September 1993.[23] Nonetheless, the effort has just begun. The Convention remains a prime example of the work that can be done with regional associations of governments and with support from international banks such as the EBRD, even if the latter was slow to approve financing of the project.

The United States needs to take the lead in developing a global consensus and an international agenda to confront the problems facing these bodies of water. A logical first step would to convene early in 1995 an international governmental-level conference (including NGOs) to address the problem of protecting both the Arctic and the Baltic seas. The intervening period should be dedicated to crash programs to further define the nature of the problem and to outline possible options. Every effort should be made to ensure that the results of the study/definition phase receive the widest public dissemination, and that there is rapid implementation of the recommendations that the conference yields.

Such an international conference, together with assistance programs, represents the kind of broadly participatory, long-term effort recommended above. It would establish the major priorities and assign specific international responsibilities in the task of cleaning up while avoiding further dumping in the Arctic Ocean, the Baltic Sea, and the Sea of Japan. Subsequent conferences could either focus on progress in meeting and achieving initial priorities or broaden the focus to examine new environmental tasks. The critical step is in formalizing an international commitment to an environmental agenda independent of the vagaries of privatization and democratization.

Turning the Red Army Green. The U.S. Department of Defense should join with the Department of Energy and with the Environmental Protection Agency to develop proposals for training and assisting the Russian military and Ministry of the Environment as they begin to undertake major environmental cleanup projects. Within the next several years Russia will have to begin cleaning up some of its most massive nuclear and chemical dumps. The armed forces should be the principal source of manpower and equipment to undertake these efforts.

"Green-helmeted" troops already have been incorporated symbolically into the structure of the Russian Armed Forces. In his first interview as head of the new Ecology and Special Protection Systems Directorate of the Russian Ministry of Defense, Colonel Sergey I. Grigorov indicated that they will be a special, noncombat unit "tasked with the function of ecological support of the Russian Army and Navy."[24]

These forces will have an active role in cleanup operations as opposed to the monitoring activities of the inspectorate* formed some eight years earlier.[25] They will be charged with cleaning up "soil and territories of test ranges, firing ranges, airfields, tank training areas, warehouses, and arsenals." The new units will organize and coordinate environmental protection for the Ministry of Defense. Disaster relief operations, such as the recovery from industrial accidents or earthquakes, will be under its jurisdiction as well. It will be assigned staff meteorologists, chemists, physicians, and other technical experts. However, at the present time, Russian military units need both training and equipment. At a roundtable held on June 16, 1993, on "Ecological Safety and the Role of the Russian Army in Ensuring It," an *Izvestiya* correspondent was told that there were only 250 inspectors in the new ecological troop service of the army. The army does not as yet train ecologists, but by implication it plans to do so.[26]

Although the interview with Colonel Grigorov took place in late 1992, implementation has taken more than a year. According to Colonel Boris Nazarov, deputy chief of the Directorate for Ecology and Special Resources, the first, experimental ecology troops were to be formed only in 1994.[27] The new troops will be attached to the Moscow Military District and to the Northern Fleet for monitoring and cleaning up areas of radioactive contamination on land and in the sea, as well as other assignments. Funding for their activities is to be provided by the sale of titanium scrap, which is strewn over "the entire tundra landscape" (presumably from booster rockets launched from the Plesetsk Cosmodrome). This ecological corps looks like a promising

---

* An Environmental Protection Department was established in the Soviet armed forces in 1980 to evaluate and repair environmental damage caused by military units in training, garrisoning, and supply activities. However, its staff was very limited, and it hardly functioned. In 1986, with Gorbachev in power, the department was reorganized, renamed as an Inspectorate for Nature Protection, placed under the control of a deputy defense minister, and had its staff cut in half almost immediately. This inspectorate was charged with the cleanup costs, and the fines were almost completely nominal during the Soviet period. Although increased environmental consciousness across the USSR was one hallmark of the period of Gorbachev's reign, the lack of support given to the inspectorate likely reflected the influence of the Soviet military, which was not behaving in an environmentally friendly way.

initiative and should be encouraged to function independent of industrial and political superstructures.

It is in the U.S. interest to prod the Russian military to provide additional military units and equipment for environmental duties. RKhM-25 chemical reconnaissance vehicles and chemical specialist troops, for example, could be assigned to ecological safety and detoxification activities. These troops, separately or integrated into the "green" troops, also could be used for emergency operations at chemical, nuclear, and microbiological industrial enterprises.[28] In addition, at some point it might be advisable for these troops to be converted into a civilian service resembling the U.S. forest rangers in order for them to be independent of any pressures from the military command that could lead to conflicts of interest.

Finally, Washington should push for an expansion of the environmental mission of the Russian military. At a meeting in the fall of 1993 convened by Yablokov as a follow-up to the original Gore-Chernomyrdin agreements in 1992 that established areas of future cooperation, there was a decision to establish an extensive array of remote sensing activities. (Backfire bombers might be used in addition to satellites to carry out some remote sensing from a lower atmospheric level.) The agreed-upon list encompasses:

- timely tracking of impending ecological disasters;

- determination of ecological disaster areas;

- reaction to emergency situations;

- tracking geological processes, such as earthquakes;

- noting land degradation;

- ice movements on rivers;

- forest diseases, pest infestation, pollution impacts on tree cover;

- pollution of surface and underground waters; and

- assisting in cartography; locating mineral deposits.

This long and valuable list requires sufficient funding "from the state budget . . . [and] users."[29] On the international level, there is room for programs such as START (Global Change System for Analysis, Research and Training) to make a contribution to the former Soviet Union. START is an environmental monitoring initiative being developed by the International Geosphere-Biosphere Programme of the International Council of Scientific Unions (ISCU) in cooperation with the World Climate Research Programme (WCRP), the International Ocean-ographic Commission of the United Nations Educational, Scientific and Cultural Organization (UNESCO), the World Meteorological Organization (WMO), and the Human Dimensions of Global Environmental Change Programme of the International Social Science Council (ISSC). The program promotes regional research centers with the aim of enhancing understanding of the regional impact of global environmental changes and furthering local scientific capacity to engage in such research.

The West's ability to influence the Russian military to assume a larger environmental mission, and to commit more manpower and material resources to it, is likely to depend on its willingness to become more deeply involved through technical and budgetary support, particularly in working with the Russian government to create and support these new "green-helmeted" forces. An early topic of conversation between NATO and its new "partners for peace" should be East-West cooperation between environmental task forces.

U.S. defense and civilian agencies need to begin to explore with the Russian government more specifically how joint environmental efforts might take place. There may be some future role for the U.S. Army Corps of Engineers in Russia, but this would necessarily have to be approached carefully, given current Russian military sensitivities.

Increased International Access to Secret Nuclear, Chemical, and Biological Warfare Facilities. Appendix B contains a list of thirty-eight secret cities that have been engaged in some form of classified defense research and development.[30] Western access and even Russian non-defense governmental access to these localities has been very limited. What has been learned raises a number of concerns: At many of these locations there is evidence of high levels of pollution, suggesting that the secret activities at those locations are contributing significantly to local health problems. Much of chemical and radioactive dumping was able to occur because of the Soviet regime's penchant for secrecy. There is also reason to suspect that budgetary problems and declining morale make these facilities vulnerable to accidents or theft of dangerous material.

Achieving international access to these facilities would contribute significantly to informing the populations of the FSU of secret activities of their own governments, such as the past efforts by Russian military authorities to hide from their own government ongoing biological and chemical activities.[31] In the case of nuclear facilities, where both the nonproliferation treaty and various bilateral agreements with the United States already provide for considerable international and national inspections, a simple agreement between Washington and Moscow could provide further guidelines for additional national or international access to each country's facilities. In the case of chemical and biological weapons research, development, and production, a stronger international agreement alone may not suffice. A new, fully independent international agency may need to be created, roughly modeled on the IAEA, but more independent of possible industry pressures, in order properly to monitor chemical and biological warfare activities. Beyond that, the NSC ought to instruct the U.S. Department of State to coordinate an intergovernmental task force looking to draw up a new series of nuclear, chemical, and biological warfare agreements explicitly related to environmental and health issues. The key requirement in the successful negotiation of new agreements will be clear conditions of mutuality. The Russian government, and the other Soviet successors, will accept further international or national inspections only to the extent that Western governments are willing to provide similar access to their facilities.

Rebuilding the Russian Forestry and National Park Services. At one time the Soviet government did a credible job in protecting the state forests and wildlife. Today, with declining budgets and plummeting morale, those who were called on to guard these national assets have become in some cases their worst plunderers. With a very small infusion of funds added for transportation, operations support, and staff salary increases, these institutions could be made effective again. Yablokov estimates that for about $200,000 a significant improvement in the Russian park service could be effectuated; since the average Russian park ranger may earn as little as $13 per month, this estimate may not be unrealistic.[32]

The U.S. Park Service should begin discussions with its Russian counterparts concerning what ways it can assist the Russian government in protecting its natural preserves. A U.S. Park Service program in Russia could be administered by the Peace Corps, as is the case in Botswana.

Remote Sensing of the Russian Forests. While at first glance this issue would seem to be of lesser priority than nuclear and chemical issues, the global implications may be even greater. The extent of the forestry losses in Russia is not really known; there is considerable belief that Russian data significantly underreports the damage to those forests. The quickest and most reliable data is from satellite photography.

NASA, as part of its overall global ecological mandate, should begin a detailed and comprehensive watch on Russian forest resources. Results should be provided in annual public reports.

TASK TWO: TREAT THE HEALTH CRISIS AS A MAJOR HUMAN CATASTROPHE

Since it will take the West and the successor governments decades to make progress on the major environmental problems inherited from the old Soviet regime, it is even more important, for both humanitarian and political reasons, to address the health crisis now. It is, in fact, a major catastrophe, every bit as deserving of international support as the 1988 earthquake in Armenia. In Russia even the most optimistic projections made by the State Statistical Agency say that deaths will exceed births in the entire Russian Federation until the second decade of the new millenium. Such a situation exists in no other industrial society.

HOW THE WEST CAN CONTRIBUTE TO PUBLIC HEALTH

Much of the Western public-health effort can and should be focused on short-run and humanitarian projects where practitioners have considerable experience; such contributions would be highly welcomed by the local population. At the same time Westerners must also provide a foundation for Russian self-help in the medium and long term. Projects should be chosen based on whether or not the resources backing them can reach the widest possible extent of the population and whether or not they can produce visible results. If pilot or demonstration projects are to be implemented, they should be chosen to demonstrate that dramatic changes can be made in people's lives.[33] People will support what they can actually see, feel, and taste. Where possible the focus should be on the creation of partnerships that combine Western skills, experience, and capital with local manpower and domestic institutional support. What the West accomplishes will be less important than what it leaves behind. Our goal is essentially political.

This health crisis, whatever its origins, is real and immediate. The West needs to respond for both humanitarian and political reasons. There is much that can be done to help. Most of it will not require major outlays in order to reap significant dividends.

International Immunization Initiative. A multinational immunization campaign, using an alliance of Western and local medical agencies operating under the authority of host governments, will work best. The principal contribution of the West (with the United States taking the lead) should be free vaccines, disposable syringes and needles, and other rudimentary medical equipment, plus a small, in-country contingent of doctors and technical staff to ensure program integrity. U.S. medical personnel could be administered through the Peace Corps.

The international assistance could be parceled out along regional lines or among several republics of the FSU, with donor countries becoming responsible for particular areas. The receiving country should be responsible for transportation of supplies and personnel and for the overall implementation of the program. Where appropriate, local partnerships should be encouraged, utilizing resources and staff of the Ministries of Health and Defense and volunteer (Red Cross) organizations. The primary objective should be to immunize every child up to the age of sixteen and every woman of childbearing age in the FSU over the next three years.

Multinational Donor Share: $5–10 million.[34]

Basic Medical Kit for Rural Health Clinics. The need for disposable syringes and needles has already been mentioned. Syringes and basic medicines apparently are now more readily available on the open markets in Moscow, St. Petersburg, and certain other cities; however, the situation outside of major urban centers and for those who cannot afford imported medical supplies is grim. In addition, there is an urgent need for basic diagnostic equipment such as stethoscopes, gynecological mirrors, blood pressure devices, and devices for blood transfusion, blood matching, diabetes monitoring, and urinalysis. In some areas available electrocardiograph equipment cannot be used because of the absence of paper and diagnostic training.

WHO drug analysts have created a list of essential drugs and supplies (Appendix C lists some seventy-five items) for the former Soviet Union. From this master list UNICEF/WHO derived, as part of its study of the looming health crisis for women and children in Kyrgyzstan, a shorter list of the highest-priority (Expanded Program on Immunization, or EPI) vaccines, drugs, and basic surgical supplies designated to meet the requirements for combatting the most common and life-threatening diseases of children (diarrhea, dysentery, and respiratory illnesses) and the most important communicable disease affecting adults (tuberculosis), for treatment of the most prevalent health problems of women (anemia and birth control), and for basic resuscitation equipment for newborns.[35]

WHO's master list, modified as it was for Kyrgyzstan, could provide a blueprint for the major international humanitarian effort needed to supply pharmaceuticals to all the states of the former Soviet Union. It needs, however, to be supplemented with basic vitamins. Vitamization is essential. On paper, their vitamization program looks good, but in reality all vitamins—from the B-complex (particularly folic acid) to vitamin D—are in great deficit. An appropriate U.S. share of this plan would be a commitment to fund, in cooperation with international agencies such as EBRD or the European Community, a priority list of essential medicines and supplies for all of Russia's children up to the age of five, plus IUDs and reproductive health supplies.

U.S. Program: $5 million.[36]

Regional Diagnostic and Training Centers. Another proposal worthy of recommendation is the establishment of no fewer than twenty-five regional diagnostic and health training centers, fully equipped with MRIs, CAT scanning machines, and nuclear resonance equipment. Modern Western equipment, however, is less important than the training that should go along with it. For this, and for all similar programs, training should come first. Therefore, these centers would best be located throughout the eleven time zones of the FSU, in close association with American teaching hospitals that can begin to introduce Western medicinal practices. The training could include everything from the use of uncomplicated diagnostic equipment to basic sanitary procedures necessary to prevent streptococcal infections, which are currently found at virtually all Russian medical and childcare institutions.

These centers should be developed through "health-care partnerships" modeled on the American International Health Alliance (AIHA) programs already in place in the FSU: in December 1992 eleven pairings were operating as sister hospitals; by July 1994 the number of partnerships had increased to twenty-one.[37] U.S. teaching hospitals should guide the partnership process from the analysis of needs through the creation of training programs. Russia's partner training institutions could be created on the basis of an existing organization, the Rosmedsotsekoninform (Russian Medical Social Economic Information Organization of the Ministry of Health, a kind of incipient National Institute of Health) under the leadership of Dr. Yuri Komarov.

Considerable savings might be achieved through the procurement in the West of older medical equipment that sits unused. There are large quantities of stockpiled devices only one generation old that remain perfectly adequate but are no longer marketable in the West because of newer, more sophisticated equipment. They can be purchased at major cost reductions, yet they represent a tremendous improvement in the average quality of equipment available to most medical facilities in the former Soviet Union. The United States could contribute by establishing a pilot project for such Regional Diagnostic and Training Centers.

U.S. Program: $20 million.

Water Purification Projects at Medical Facilities. Throughout the former Soviet Union there is an urgent need to provide clean water to medical facilities. The United States can provide immediate help through technical assistance and in some cases offering up-to-date water filtration equipment that is not currently universally available within the FSU. These do not have to be very large installations. Even small-capacity equipment would be a major improvement in a vast number of smaller hospitals, polyclinics, and rural medical facilities.

U.S. Program: $5–10 million.[38]

TASK THREE: BUILD HEALTH AND ECOLOGY ALLIANCES

Neglect, combined with a series of government acts undertaken over decades, created the current crisis. It will take a set of new actions by the successor governments to the Soviet Union to begin the process of cleanup and maintain it subsequently. The United States can do a great deal with relatively little money to strengthen the hand of those inside and out of the government who are concerned with the ecological and health problems facing these new states. The overall objective is to identify and assist indigenous institutions that can act as a safeguard of the nation's health and ecology. Thanks to AID assistance and the work of ISAR, a firm foundation has been established for environmental NGOs in the successor states, but less has been achieved to activate NGOs in the field of health. More attention should be paid to laying the groundwork of health politics, with special consideration given to lobbies for maternal and child health.

The basic policy objectives of the West need not be complicated, controversial, or costly: For example, Western aid programs in Russia should aim to achieve proper water purity standards. Such standards should be reasonable, enforceable, and applicable to all agencies, civilian and military; after all, those that are so stringent that they cannot be attained are, as a result, ignored. Another objective might be the adoption of new regulations in the use of pesticides. Western aid projects need not be large in scale to achieve such regulatory policy objectives. Individual countries and international agencies can contribute much to this program.[39]

CHANGING THE BUREAUCRATIC CULTURE AND RAISING ENVIRONMENTAL AWARENESS

Efforts over the last several years to encourage sound environmental and health practices in the FSU have been hindered by the policies and practices of the past; the end of the Soviet regime has not meant the end of a Soviet culture and bureaucracy that rewarded production at the expense of environmental considerations. The four most common attitudes of Soviet bureaucracy were: make it big; keep it secret; meet production quotas at any cost; reward many for success but make no one responsible for failure. Today this mentality lives on in countless dingy government offices.

The Soviet bureaucratic legacy of excessive centralization continues to inhibit practical and realistic environmental and health initiatives. Information still flows upward and is rarely shared laterally. Conflicting jurisdictions between ministries and agencies and among center, oblast, *rayon,* and municipal authorities discourage individual initiative at all levels.

The first central government committee to regulate and enforce environmental policy and to coordinate the work of ministries and committees responsible for environmental management and nature protection was authorized in 1987 and formed only in 1988. The first official reports on industrial toxic waste, based on existing data, were published only in 1990. The new Russian government passed its first environmental protection law in 1991; the law provides a legal framework for local authorities to assess pollution damage and slap fines on local polluters, but it is not clear how effective regulatory enforcement will be. Today, permissible pollution limits are exceeded without a thought. When fines have been levied, the weakened ruble has made them a joke.[40]

What has changed is that there is a new health and environmental awareness throughout the FSU. In spite of the poor showing of the "Green" Party during the 1993 Duma election (they failed to win even one seat, suggesting that most Russians still consider other issues as being more important for now), Russian environmentalists are better organized than at any time in the past. And since April 1994 the "Green" movements have been joined by a new "White" movement, initiated by Andrey Demin, a leading Russian health specialist on Yablokov's staff, to lobby on health issues.[41] These constituencies have a major representative on the Russian Federation's Security Council in Yablokov himself. The Ministry of the Environment has counterpart Environmental councils (*ekologicheskiye sovety*) at all levels down to the oblast. Most recently their increased strength was demonstrated when a local environmental council sued the military authorities of the Plesetsk Cosmodrome and forced them to admit to environmentally harmful practices in the use of heptyl. New nongovernmental environmental groups have sprung up in recent years, although some single-issue NGOs disband after succeeding or failing in their confrontation with authorities, enterprises, or the like. Private environmental groups have successfully blocked some of the more destructive Korean timber practices in Siberia.

The most important recent environmental initiative in Moscow was the proposal of the Russian Environment Ministry in February 1992 to launch a "Russian Federation Environmental Security" plan. This is an extremely ambitious effort to set up systematic reporting and analysis to monitor all threats to the Russian environment. In designing a draft environmental security system,[42] the Environment Ministry has established a catchall set of environmental monitoring priorities designed to reveal the underlying causes of the wasteful use of natural resources and pollution so that these practices can be modified. The proposed monitoring system—if it does not overwhelm those very ministries and agencies that have been assigned to implement the program—is necessary but probably not sufficient to prevent further environmental deterioration. At minimum the environmental survey resulting from all this observation and analysis should provide a more accurate assessment of environmental damage and its impact on public health.

The survey will include specific data on dumping, industrial pollution, and health statistics; it will also focus on more complex issues such as "changes in biological balance," undesirable pathogenic mutations, and saprophytic microorganisms. The survey should for the first time give the Russian policymaker a much better handle on the activities of the Ministries of Defense and Atomic Energy and various secret facilities. The heart of the survey program would be the data obtained from the Unified State Monitoring System, and would incorporate monitoring of:

- medical facilities;

- industrial, energy-related, and transportation facilities;

- nuclear power facilities;

- potentially hazardous sites;

- hazardous chemical, radioactive, or biological wastes, particularly storage and burial sites;

- hazardous material shipments;

- production and household wastes;

- seismic activity and volcanoes;

- global natural phenomena and processes;

- agricultural production; and

- soils and land.

To make the environmental security system operational, international donors will be needed to provide computer equipment and other material support at the national and local (oblast) levels.

U.S. Contributions to Environmental Surveillance and Public Information

There are a number of specific ways in which the United States can support this important initiative.

Proposal: Equip a Federal Information and Analysis Center, Regional Information and Analysis Centers, and Local (Oblast) Ecology Committees. The critical organizational entities needed in Russia to implement the proposed environmental security system will be a Federal Information and Analysis Center, the Regional Information and Analysis Centers, and most importantly the eighty-eight oblast environmental committees. Both the federal and regional centers are proposed new entities that will need to be staffed and equipped. It is in the United States' interest, as well as in the interest of the West, interest to insure that these bodies have the best equipment and training possible to guarantee that the data and analysis generated meet international standards and are accurate and timely.

The eighty-eight oblast environmental committees are operating with very inadequate budgets and little office equipment. They urgently need computers with modems, fax machines, and copying machines. The EPA, in cooperation with the Russian Ministry of Environment, should develop a program to upgrade the proficiency of these committees, whereby the provision of Western equipment and technical training would be matched with increased local funding for operations and training. A major goal of the program should be to link health and environmental groups at the oblast and higher levels of government, as well as concerned nongovernmental organizations, through electronic information systems.

U.S. Program: $3–5 million[43]

Proposal: Daily Television Program Dedicated To Health and Environmental Issues. The United States should grant technical support to one pilot project, probably in Russia, to provide public information on health and environmental issues by means of a daily, one-hour television program. The program could be used to highlight and commend important steps toward improving waste disposal or filtering of emissions and to focus attention on major medical and ecological disasters as they develop. The program could include a wide variety of other issues: general sanitation problems, personal hygiene, outbreaks of infectious diseases, reports of unsafe food and water, and pollution indices.

U.S. Program: $1 million.[44]

Proposal: Utilize Research Capabilities of Nongovernmental Organizations. It is vital to mobilize the energy of nongovernmental environmental and health organizations to do research and act as indigenous watchdogs. The most direct way for the United States to achieve this objective would be to establish an annual fund, administered by the EPA or some interagency group, to support contracts for specific small research projects.[45] The principal umbrella organization in Russia today continues to be the Socio-Ecological Union and its Center for Independent Ecological Programs (CIEP). The CIEP has contacts with two to three hundred environmental groups throughout the FSU. Its own staff has proposed conducting research in various fields, such as ecologically related illness; toxic waste; energy and the environment, especially the nuclear industry's impact on ecology; environmental education; biodiversity and protected nature reserves; organic farming; information services through its own International Clearinghouse on the Environment; ecotourism; and regional socio-ecological projects.[46] Expanded funding for this group is highly recommended, with the clear understanding that the research conducted by CIEP meets international expectations for rigor, objectivity, and sound methodology. Another nongovernmental organization worthy of support is Dr. Yablokov's Center for Ecological Policy. It is reasonable to anticipate that most project costs would be small—in the $25,000 to $50,000 range—and projects could be conducted in alliance with U.S. organizations to ensure oversight for the sake of quality and to strengthen international links. This proposal, if implemented, would increase Western scientific understanding on a number of key policy fronts. However, the real payoff would be the empowerment of indigenous environmental and health groups.

U.S. Program (annual): $250,000.

AFTERWORD

The environmental and health crisis of former Soviet Union presents an agenda both immense and daunting. It is impossible in a study of this size to describe adequately the damage inflicted on the people of the region; it is even less possible to provide the complete and final blueprint for recovery. Not every issue has been dealt with; not all the problems identified have been fully explored. This paper has cited some indices of pollution, but it has not done more than scratch the surface of the growing accumulation of data that links significant health problems in the population to this pollution. It contains only the briefest description of all the adverse conditions that have produced a declining population—a population in danger of destroying the quality of its own genetic stock. Most importantly, this study been reticent in prescribing answers. The answers—if it is ever possible to construct a clear policy prescription—will require much more data and a great deal more study.

"Possibly the best we can do right now is to buy time." This was the considered judgment of the Bellona Foundation's head of research, Frederic Hauge, a leading Norwegian environmentalist, a student of Russia, and a frequent visitor in recent years to that country.[1] Early efforts to provide assistance were often poorly thought out and failed in their intent or were abandoned before fulfillment. Hard realities have often forced Western governments to rethink aid plans. It may be impossible, or even counterproductive, for Western governments to try to clean up a nickel plant (a notorious polluter) that is located far from both its raw materials and its market, is equipped with outdated, inefficient machinery, and is administered with apathetic, Soviet-style attitudes toward pollution abatement and maintenance of capital stock. A better solution may just be to close the plant and move the workers as well as production to a new location with cleaner facilities. However, no government or private concern is prepared to recommend and finance such a radical solution within the near future.

Nevertheless, there is potential for a watershed transformation in the underlying politics that will affect future governmental actions throughout the Former Soviet Union. A new awareness that environmental and health problems constitute a serious national security issue is reflected in Article 7 of the State Secrets Act of 1994, in President Yeltsin's 1993 decree establishing a nuclear inventory following the Tomsk-7 accident, in the Yablokov Commission Reports, in the formation of the new Interagency Environmental Security Committee of the Russian National Security Council, in the release of data such as those provided by the Vorfolomeyev Committee, in the Sakha (formerly called Yakutiya) Republic's publication of the health impact on its population of the twelve "peaceful" atomic explosions on its territory by the Soviet government, and in numerous other official and unofficial revelations contained in Socio-Ecological Union publications. With minimal Western encouragement, backed by strategically focused resources, the opportunity exists to increase dramatically global understanding of the crisis, to change the nature of political debate within the FSU, and to enhance the possibility of implementing environmentally sound, health-sensitive policies.

What the West needs at this point is not a detailed blueprint for future action, but a new intellectual framework for approaching the problem: Patience is necessary. More importantly, policymakers must think in terms of multiyear time frames, collective action, mechanisms for developing joint Western strategies, and coordination.

It is essential as well to think in terms of local partnerships. All efforts should be focused on strengthening local institutions and building political support at the grass roots. Training programs should have the highest priority. Cooperative action and burden sharing should be the centerpiece of every project. Providing or selling U.S. equipment is not the goal; empowering local institutions or organizations to tackle critical problems is. The West needs to give a focus to all of its projects. Objectives should not be only measurable but visible to the average citizen.

Above all, we need to reconnect with the people of Eurasia from whom we have been estranged during a half century of cold war. For this reason health and humanitarian issues belong at the center of all our projects. The theme that unites all Western efforts should be shared humanity and shared habitation of the same planet.

APPENDIXES

APPENDIX A[1]

SECRET AND CLOSED CITIES

SECRET NAME	LOCAL NAME	OBLAST/KRAY/ASSR[2]
Alkino-2	(NA)[3]	*Bashkortostan*
Arzamas-16	Kremlev	Nizhegorodskaya obl.
Bologoe-4	Ozernyy	Tverskaya obl.
Chelyabinsk-65	Ozersk	Chelyabinskaya obl.
Chelyabisnk-70	Snezhinsk	Chelyabinskaya obl.
Chelyabinsk-95	(NA)	(NA)
Chelyabinsk-115	(NA)	(NA)
Chita-46	*Gornyy*	*Chitinskaya obl.*
Dombrovskiy-3	Komarovskiy	Orenburgskaya obl.
Golitsyno-2	Krasnoznamensk	Moskovskaya obl.
Kapustin-Yar-1	Znamensk	Astrakhanskaya obl.
Kartaly-6	Lokomotovnyy	Chelyabinskaya obl.
Kosulino-1	Ural'skiy	Sverdlovskaya obl.
Krasnoyarsk-25	(NA)	(NA)
Krasnoyarsk-26	Zheleznogorsk	Krasnoyarskiy *kray*
Krasnoyarsk-35	Podgornyy	Krasnoyarskiy *kray*
Krasnoyarsk-45	Zelenogorsk	Krasnoyarskiy *kray*
Krasnoyarsk-66	Kedrovyy	Krasnoyarskiy *kray*
Krasnoyarsk-95	(NA)	(NA)
Kurchatov-21	(NA)	*Semipalatinskaya obl.*
		(Kazakhstan)
Mirnyy	Mirnyy	Arkhangel'skaya obl.
Moscow-21	(NA)	*Semipalatinskaya obl.*
		(Kazakhstan)
Moscow-400	(NA)	*Semipalatinskaya obl.*
		(Kazakhstan)
Murmansk-60	Snezhogorsk	Murmanskaya obl.
Murmansk-130	Skalistyy	Murmanskaya obl.
Murmansk-140	Ostrovnoy	Murmanskaya obl.
Murmansk-150	Zaozersk	Murmanskaya obl.
Naro-Fominsk-5	Molodezhnyy	Moskovskaya obl.
Novopetrovsk-2	Voskhod	Moskovskaya obl.
Nizhniy-Tagil-39	Svobodnyy	Sverdlovskaya obl.
Olovyannaya-4	(NA)	Chitinskaya obl.
Penza-19	Zarechnyy	Penzenskaya obl.
Perm'-76	Zvezdnyy	Permskaya obl.
Petropavlovsk-Kamchatskiy-35	Vulkanniy	Kamchatskaya obl.

Secret Name	Local Name	Oblast/Kray/ASSR[4]
Petropavlovsk Kamchatskiy-50	Vilyuchinsk	Kamchatskaya obl.
Plesetsk	Plesetsk	Murmanskaya obl.
Semipalatinsk-121	*Kurchatov*	*Semipalatinskaya obl. (Kazakhstan)*
Severodvinsk	Severodvinsk	Arkhangelskaya obl.
Shkotovo-17	Fokino	Primorskiy *kray*
Shkotovo-22	Dunai	Primorskiy *kray*
Shkotovo-26	Putyatin	Primorskiy *kray*
Sosnovoborsk	(NA)	(NA)
Stupino-7	Prioksk	Moskovskaya obl.
Sverdlovsk-44	Novoural'sk	Sverdlovskaya obl.
Sverdlovsk-45	Lesnoy	Sverdlovskaya obl.
Svobodnyy-18	Ugelgorsk	Amurskaya obl.
Tatishchevo-5	Svetlyy	Saratovskaya obl.
Tomsk-7	Seversk	Tomskaya obl.
Uzhur-4	Solnechnyy	Krasnoyarskiy *kray*
Yur'ya-2	Pervomayskiy	Kirovskaya obl.
Zagorsk-7	(NA)	(NA)
Zlatoust-20[5]	*Trekhgornyy*	*Chelyabinskaya obl.*
Zlatoust-36	Trekhgornyy	Chelyabinskaya obl.

[1] Cities in italics are mentioned in only one source; all other cities have appeared in at least two different sources
[2] In the Russian Federation unless otherwise indicate
[3] NA = Not available
[4] Unless otherwise indicated
[5] Probably the same as Zlatoust-36

APPENDIX B

CHEMICAL WEAPONS INDUSTRY CITY LIST

NAME	TYPE	PRODUCT(S)
Aleksin	P	mustard gas
Asha	P	mustard gas, lewisite, adamsite
Astrakhan	T	(NA)
Berezniki	P	mustard gas, lewisite, adamsite, di-phenol-chlorarsine
Chapayevsk	S, P	mustard gas, lewisite
Chita	S	(NA)
Dzerzhinsk	S, P	mustard gas, lewisite
Efremov	P	mustard gas
Florishchi	T	(NA)
Gelendzhik	T	(NA)
Gornyy	S	mustard gas, lewisite
Gorokhovets	S, T	(NA)
Groznyy	P	di-phenol-chlorarsine
Irbit	P	adamsite
Irkutsk	S	(NA)
Kambarka	S	(NA)
Kazan'	P	mustard gas
Kemerovo	P	mustard gas, lewisite, adamsite
Kineshma	P	adamsite
Kirov	S	(NA)
Kirovsk	P	mustard gas
Kizner	S	phosphorous
Komsomol'sk	S	(NA)
Krasnoyarsk	S	(NA)
Leonidovka	S	phosphorous
Lipetsk	S	(NA)
Luga	T	(NA)
Maradykovskiy	S	phosphorous
Magnitogorsk	P	mustard gas
Mendeleyevsk	P	mustard gas
Moscow	S, T, P	mustard gas, lewisite, di-phenol-chlorarsine
Nizhniy Tagil	P	mustard gas, adamsite
Novocheboksarsk	P	phosphorous
Novomoskovsk	P	mustard gas, lewisite, adamite
Omsk	P	mustard gas
Petrozavodsk	P	mustard gas

NAME	TYPE	PRODUCT(S)
Pochep	S	phosphorous
Saratov	S, T	(NA)
Shchelkovo	P	mustard gas, di-phenol-chlorarsine
Shchuch'ye	S	phosphorous
Shikhany (Shikhany-1)	S, T	irritants
Slavgorod	P	irritants
St. Petersburg	P	mustard gas
Syzran'	S	(NA)
Tomsk	P	mustard gas, lewisite, adamsite
Turinsk	P	adamsite
Usol'ye	S	(NA)
Usol'ye-Sibirskoye	P	mustard gas
Ussuriysk	S	(NA)
Vladivostok	T	(NA)
Volgograd	S, P	phosphorous
Vol'sk-17	P	irritants
Voskresensk	P	mustard gas, lewisite

S = Storage Facility (23)
T = Testing Facility (9)
P = Production Facility (29)

Source: Vil Mirzayanov, "Ekologiya i Konversiya", in Socio-Ecological Union, *Khimicheskoe oruzhiye: Problemy unichtozheniya,* Spetsvypusk, October 1993, pp. 10–11.

APPENDIX C

LIST OF PRIORITY DRUGS AND ESTIMATED COSTS
(6 MONTHS SUPPLY FOR 5 MILLION POPULATION)

EDL No.	Drug	Price/ Package	No. of Packages	Total Price US$
1.1	Diazepam inj.	7/100	100	700
1.2	Ketamini inj. 50 mg	100/100	100	10,000
1.3	Lidocaine inj. 2%	10/100	4,000	40,000
2	Diclofenac inj.	25/100	100	2,500
3.1	Dexamethasone inj. 4 mg	15/100	100	1,500
3.2	Prednisolone tab. 5 mg	10/100	100	1,000
6.1	Levamisole 150 mg	13/1000	100	1,300
6.2.1	Ampicillin inj. 500 mg.	25/100	1,000	25,000
6.2.1	Ampicillin inj. 250 mg	20/100	1,500	30,000
6.2.1	Benzylpenicillin sodium 5 mill. IU	45/100	1,000	45,000
6.2.1	Phenoxymethylpenicillin tab. 250 mg	15/1000	7,000	15,000
6.2.2	Gentamicin inj. 10 mg	12/100	1,000	12,000
6.2.2	Gentamicin inj. 40 mg	15/100	1,000	15,000
6.2.2	Metronidazole inj. 500 mg	100/100	200	20,000
6.2.2	Co-trimazol tab. 100 mg + 20 mg	7/1000	500	3,500
6.2.2	Co-trimazol tab. 3400 mg + 80 mg	16/1000	500	8,000
6.2.2	Cefazoline inj. 0.25 or eqv. cure (Ketzol)	30/cure	2,000	60,000
6.2.2	Cefazoline inj. 0.50 or eqv. cure (Ketzol)	30/cure	2,000	60,000
6.2.2	Tetracycline tab.	15/1000	1,500	22,500
6.2.4	Ethambutol 400 mg	25/1000	10	250
6.2.4	Rifampicin 150 mg	50/1000	10	500
6.2.4	Rifampicin + Isoniazid 150 mg	55/1000	10	550
6.3	Nystatin tab.	40/1000	10	400
6.2	Nystatin pessary	4/100	20	80
8.2	Vincristine inj. 5 mg	600/100	12	12,000
8.3	Tamoxifen tab. 10 mg 100 tab	40/1	100	4,000
10.1	Ferrous salt tab 60 mg	2/1000	2,000	4,000
10.1	Ferrous + folic acid tab.	2/1000	2/1000	4,000
10.2	Heparin inj. 5000 IU-5 ml	220/100	50	11,000
10.2	Protamin sulfate inj. 10 mg	110/100	10	1,100

EDL No.		PRICE/ PACKAGE	NO. OF PACKAGES	TOTAL Price US$
11.1	Dextran 70–76% infusion	8/1	5,000	40,000
12.1	Glyceryl trinitrate 0.5 mg	10/1000	50	500
12.1	Nifedipin tab. 40 mg	28/1000	10	280
12.1	Propranolol inj. 1 mg	10/100	50	500
12.2	Verapamil tab. 40 mg	7/1000	200	1,400
12.2	Verapamil tab. 80 mg	9/1000	200	1,800
12.4	Digoxin inj. 10 mg	27/100	30	800
16	Furosemide inj. 10 mg	10/100	100	1,000
16	Furosemide tab. 40 mg	7/1000	100	700
17.1	Aluminum Hydroxide susp.	4/1	20,000	80,000
17.1	Cimetidine tab. 200 mg	40/1000	100	4,000
17.1	Cimetidine inj. 200 mg	14/100	50	700
17.2	Metoclopramide tab. 10 mg	7/1000	50	350
17.2	Metoclopramide inj. 5 mg	15/100	30	450
18.5	Insulin 40 IU/ml	250/100	100	25,000
18.5	Insulin 40 IU/ml, intermd.	250/100	100	25,000
21.2	Pilocarpine eye drops	100/100	100	10,000
21.4	Timolol	/100	10	
22.1	Ergometrine inj.	13/100	50	750
22.1	Oxytocin inj.	13/100	1,500	19,500
24	Amitriptyline inj. 10 mg	9/100	200	1,800
24	Amitriptyline inj. 10 mg	7/1000	10	70
24	Haloperidol tab. 5 mg	7/1000	5	35
24	Haloperidol tab. 5 mg	20/100	150	3,000
25.1	Beclometasone Aerosol	2/1	1,000	2,000
25.1	Salbutamol Aerosol	2/1	30,000	60,000
25.1	Aminophylline inj. 25 mg	12/100	50	600
25.1	Aminophylline inj. 200 mg	10/1000	20	200
26.2	Glucose 5%	2/1	10,000	20,000
26.2	Potassium Chloride 1.5 mmol	1/1	1,000	1,000
26.2	Sodium Bicarbonate 1.4%	2/1	1,000	2,000
26.2	Sodium Chloride 0.9%	2/1	50,000	100,000
	50% Freight, Charges etc.			447,147
	Total			1,320,492

Source: United Nations, International Children's Emergency Fund, *The Looming Crisis of Children and Women in Kyrgyzstan: Report of a UNICEF/WHO Collaborative Mission with the Participation of UNDP, UNFPA, WFP,* February 21–26, 1992, Annex List B, pp. 1–3.

APPENDIX D
AIHA HEALTH-CARE PARTNERSHIPS

HOSPITAL NAME	LOCATION	U.S. PARTNER
Emergency Hospital	Yerevan, Armenia	Boston University School of Medicine, Boston University Medical Center Hospital, Boston, (MA)
Women's Reproductive Health Center and Erebuni Hospital	Yerevan, Armenia	Beth Israel Hospital, Harvard Medical Alumni Association (Boston, MA)
Fourth Hospital for Sick Children, Radiation Medicine Institute, Minsk Medical Institute	Minsk, Belarus	Children's Hospital of Pittsburgh (Pittsburgh, PA)
City Hospital No. 2, State Medical Institute	Tbilisi, Georgia	Grady Memorial Hospital, Emory University School of Medicine, Morehouse School of Medicine, (Atlanta, GA)
Kazakh Scientific Research Institute for Pediatrics, Almaty, First Aid Hopital	Almaty, Kazakhstan	Tucson/Almaty Health Care Coalition of 8 Hospitals (Tuscon, AZ)
Institute of Obstetrics and Pediatrics, Institute of Oncology and Radiology	Bishkek, Kyrgyzstan	University of Kansas Medical Center (Kansas City, KS)
Republican Clinical Hospital, City Ambulance Center	Chisinau, Moldova	Hennepin County Medical Center and Health Span (Minneapolis, MN)
City Hospital No. 2, Vladivostok Medical Institute	Vladivostok, Russia	Medical College of Virginia/ Virginia Commonwealth University (Richmond, VA)
First Medical Institute in the name of Pavlov, Medical Sanitary Unit No. 122	St. Petersburg, Russia	Jewish Hospital (Louisville, KY), University of Louisville School of Medicine and the Georgia Baptist Medical Center (Atlanta, GA)

Governmental Medical center of the Russian Federation/Kuntsevo	Moscow, Russia	Premier Health Alliance, Inc., (Chicago, IL)
Hospital No. 9, Hospital No.166, Bolshaya Volga Hospital	Dubna, Russia	Lutheran Hospital, St. Francis Hospital (LaCrosse, WI)
Municipal Hospital No. 1	Moscow, Russia	Brigham and Women's Hospital (Boston, MA)
Murmansk Regional Hospital, City Ambulance Hospital	Murmansk, Russia	St. Vincent's Medical Center, Memorial Medical Center (Jacksonville, FL)
Savior's Hospital for Peace and Charity	Moscow, Russia	Magee Women's Hospital (Pittsburgh, PA)
Stavropol Regional Hospital	Stavropol, Russia	Mercy Hospital, Iowa Hospital Association (Cedar Rapids, IA)
Children's Hospital No. 2, Obstetrical Hospital No. 3	Kiev, Ukraine	Children's Hospital of Philadelphia, University of Pennsylvania School of Medicine, Hospital of the University of Pennsylvania (Philadelphia, PA)
L'viv Oblast Clinical Hospital, L'viv State Medical Institute, L'viv Oblast Admin.	L'viv, Ukraine	Henry Ford Health System (Detroit, MI) Kaiser Permanente (Cleveland, OH)
Odessa Oblast Hospital	Odessa, Ukraine	Coney Island Hospital (New York, NY)
Railway Oblast Hospital, Perinatal Hospital	Kiev, Ukraine	Millard Fillmore Hospitals (Buffalo, NY)
Second State Medical Institute	Tashkent, Uzbekistan	University of Illinois Hospital (Chicago, IL)
Medical Consultative Center in the Name of President Niyazov	Ashgabat, Turkmenistan	Cleveland Clinic Foundation (Cleveland, OH)

Source: *CommonHealth*, Newsletter of the American International Health Alliance 2, no. 5 (June/July 1994): 31.

APPENDIX E

STARTUP OF ENERGY BLOCKS AT NUCLEAR POWER PLANTS IN RUSSIA: 1992 TO 2010

NAME OF PLANT, NO. OF BLOCK	CAPACITY, MEGAWATTS	1992–1995	1996–2000	2001–2005	2006–2010
Completed Construction					
Balakovo, 4	1000	x	—	—	—
Kursk, 5	1000	x	—	—	—
Kalinin, 3	1000	x	—	—	—
Replacing those Withdrawn					
Bilibino, 5	32	¦	—	x	—
Bilibino, 6	32	—	—	x	—
Bilibino, 7	32	—	—	—	x
Novovoronezh, 6	1000	—	—	x	—
Novovoronezh, 7	1000	—	—	x	—
Kola, 5	630	—	—	x	—
Kola, 6	630	—	—	x	—
Kola, 7	630	—	—	—	x
New Energy Blocks					
Balakovo, 5	1000	—	x	—	—
Balakovo, 6	1000	—	—	x	—
Voronezh Nuclear Heat Supply Plant, 1	500	—	—	x	—
Voronezh Nuclear Heat Supply Plant, 2	500	—	x	—	—
South Ural, 1	800	—	x	—	—

South Ural, 2	800	—	—	x	—
South Ural, 3	800	—	x	x	x
Beloyarsk, 4	800	—	x	—	—
New Nuclear Power Plants and Nuclear Heat Supply Plants					
Far Eastern, 1	600	—	—	x	—
Far Eastern, 2	600	—	—	—	x
Maritime, 1	600	—	—	x	—
Maritime, 2	600	—	—	—	x
Khabarovsk Nuclear Heat Supply Plant, 1	500	—	—	x	—
Khabarovsk Nuclear Heat Supply Plant, 2	500	—	—	x	x
Sosnovy Bor, 1	530	—	x	—	—
Storage of Spent Nuclear Fuel					
Smolensk (Spent Nuclear Fuel Storage Facility)		x	—	—	—
Total		4	6	13	4

Source: S. Leskov, "Nuclear Energy Program Enjoying Renewed Optimism," *Izvestiya,* February 6, 1993, pp. 1, 5, translated in Foreign Broadcast Information Service, *FBIS Report: Central Eurasia,* FBIS-USR-93-017, February 13, 1993, p. 44.

APPENDIX F

TOTAL RELEASE OF METALS INTO THE ATMOSPHERE: 1992
(Thousands of tons per year)

SUBSTANCE	SOURCE			TOTAL RELEASE		RATIO (IN %)
	Industry	Power Stations	Motor Vehicles	Russia	EEC	
Arsenic	1.7000	0.4	—	2.100	0.278	755.4
Cadmium	0.0110	0.4	—	0.410	0.004	10,250.0
Copper	5.9000	1.3	—	7.200	0.061	11,803.2
Hydrogen Fluoride	15.4000	3.5	—	18.900	—	—
Lead	2.0600	0.9	2.0	5.000	0.295	1,694.9
Manganese	2.8000	1.0	—	3.800	—	—
Mercury	0.0008	0.2	—	0.028	—	—
Nickel	5.0000	1.8	—	6.800	0.108	6,296.3
Vanadium	5.1000	12.0	—	17.100	0.212	8,066.0
Zinc	—	3.0	—	3.000	—	—

Source: B. A. Revich, *Zagryazneniye vozdukha gorodov i zdorov'ye detskogo naseleniya,* Issue no. 11, Institut Prognozirovaniya RAN, Moscow, December 1993, p. 6. Ratio of total release in Russia and the EEC were derived from data in the original source.

NOTES

INTRODUCTION

1. State Report on the State of the Environment of the Russian Federation in 1992, *Zelenyy mir* (Moscow), nos. 19–27 (Aug. 25–Nov. 23, 1993), translated in Joint Publications Research Service (hereafter "JPRS"), *JPRS Report, Environmental Issues,* JPRS-TEN-94-005, February 25, 1994, p. 1.

2. Murray Feshbach and Alfred Friendly, Jr., *Ecocide in the USSR: Health and Nature Under Siege* (New York: Basic Books, 1992), p. 1.

3. Yablokov has on several occasions questioned the completeness and accuracy of information provided by the Russian military.

4. V. P. Vorfolomeyev, "Ekologicheskaya bezopasnost' segodnya—s uchetom ekonomicheskikh realiy" (Ecological Security Today: Taking into Account Economic Realities"), *Zelenyy mir* (Moscow) no. 3, (February 1, 1993): 4.

5. Mayak Radio Network (Moscow), March 13, 1993, translated in JPRS, *JPRS Report, Environmental Issues,* JPRS-TEN-93-010, April 20, 1993, p. 21. In the 1980s the number of nuclear research installations in Moscow climbed to fifty-two. That number has now dropped to forty, half of which are in operation no more than three months a year. See "Nuclear Waste Piling Up in Moscow," *Izvestiya* (Moscow), July 13, 1994, p. 11, translated in JPRS, *JPRS Report, Environmental Issues,* JPRS-TEN-94-019, August 5, 1994, p. 43.

6. Vlad Ignatov and Vera Romanova, "Russia's Nuclear Facilities Inventoried: Absolutely No Order," *Segodnya* (Moscow), February 1994, p. 9, translated in JPRS, *JPRS Report, Science & Technology,* JPRS-UST-94-008, March 31, 1994, p. 48.

7. Igor Dvinsky, "The Pacific Fleet's Radioactive Storage Site Begins to 'Glare,'" *Segodnya* (Moscow), June 28, 1994. I am indebted to Joshua Handler of Greenpeace for providing me with this translation.

8. Cited by Interfax (Moscow), April 6, 1993, translated in BBC Monitoring, *Summary of World Broadcasts, Weekly Economic Report, Former USSR,* SU/W0278, April 23 1993, p. A/23.

9. Nonetheless, more information is available about the names, locations, and activities of these secret cities, revealing that they were the backbone of the Soviet Union's military-industrial complex. The available information on secret cities and facilities is provided in Appendixes A and B. See also Thomas

B. Cochran et al., *Soviet Nuclear Weapons,* Nuclear Weapons Databook, vol. 4, issued by the National Resources Defense Council, New York, 1989, and Thomas B. Cochran and Robert Standish Norris, *Russian/Soviet Nuclear Warhead Production,* Nuclear Weapons Databook, working papers, issued by the NRDC, September 8, 1993.

10. An unpublished World Bank report, not surprisingly, has found that basic information is unreliable. In fact, it concluded that data are often based on narrow responsibilities, poor dissemination of information, "even deliberate misreporting of environmental data," and, in some cases, "the data provided was in error by factors of 2, 5 or even as much as 10. In many situations it is simply impossible to judge by how much the data are in error." World Bank, *Environmental Management: Technical Assistance Report,* September 1993, p. 21.

11. Interdepartmental Commission of the Russian Federation Security Council on Ecological Safety, "Each Person Must Decide How to Save Himself and His Children," *Rossiyskiye vesti* (Moscow), February 11, 1994, p. 4, translated in JPRS, *JPRS Report, Environmental Issues,* JPRS-TEN-94-009, April 7, 1994, pp. 25–31.

12. Julia Rubin, "Hard Times, Poor Care Blamed for 'Birth Crisis,'" Associated Press, March 16 1994.

13. Ibid.

14. Administration of the President of the Russian Federation, Ministry of Health of the Rusian Federation, Russian Academy of Medical Sciences, and the State Committee for Sanitary and Epidemological Oversight, *State Report on the State of Health of the Population of the Russian Federation in 1992,* Moscow, 1993, pp. 21–22. This is not precisely defined in the sources. It appears to relate to the number of physician visits (five or more) per year and the presence of chronic illness(es).

15. The author is indebted to Suzanne Massie, Harvard University, for this figure.

16. Interview with Galina Serdyukovskaya by I. Konchakova and V. Romenenko. "Do We Have a Future?" *Argumenty i fakty* (Moscow), no. 43 (October, 1991): 5, translated in JPRS, *JPRS Report, Life Sciences,* JPRS-ULS-92-003, January 28, 1992, pp. 29–32.

17. Ibid.

18. *Pravda* (Moscow), October 9, 1990, p. 6.

19. Rubin, "Hard Times, Poor Care."

20. Sergey Kudryashov, "Bashkiriya Hushes Up Ecological Problems," *Izvestiya* (Moscow), August 31, 1993, p. 2, translated in JPRS, *JPRS Report, Environmental Issues,* JPRS-TEN-93-026, November 24, 1993, pp. 49–50.

21. Rubin, "Hard Times, Poor Care."

22. Chrystia Freeland, "Russians 'Doomed for Next 25 Years,'" *Financial Times* (London), October 8, 1992, p. 16.

23. "Russian Government Commission Discusses Medical Supplies," BBC Monitoring, *Summary of World Broadcasts: Former USSR,* April 29, 1994, p. 9.

24. Aleksey Yurenev, "Vrachi ne znayut, kak i chem lechit" ("Doctors Don't Know How and with What to Heal,") *Rossiyskiye vesti* (Moscow), April 1, 1994, p. 5.

25. Valentina Proskurina, "Run, Rabbit, Run!" *Pravda* (Moscow), January 27, 1993, p. 4, translated in JPRS, *JPRS Report, Environmental Issues,* JPRS-TEN-93-015, pp. 59–60. The figures for child inoculations come from B. K. Tatechenko, chief of the Center for Inoculation Pathology at the Institute of Pediatrics of the Russian Academy of Medical Sciences.

26. Ninety percent of Europe's polio cases and 95 percent of its diphtheria cases have been registered in the CIS, where one-third of the population lives. Anatoliy Monisov, deputy chairman of the Sanitary-Epidemiological Inspection Commission, gave this estimate in September 1992. According to the World Health Organization's survey of 1987 data in twenty-seven countries of Europe, twenty recorded zero cases of diphtheria, eleven had no more than six cases and one (the former Soviet Union) had more than one thousand cases. See interview of Monisov by Andrey Bayduzhiy, ". . . Plus Vaccinating the Entire Country: Could Immunizations Violate Human Rights?" *Nezavisimay gazeta* (Moscow), September 24, 1992, p. 6; and S. S. Markina et al., "Epidemiologicheskaya kharakteristika difteriynoy infekstsii" ("Epidemiological Characteristics of Diphtheria Infection"), *Zdravookhraneniye Rossiyskoy Federatsii* (Moscow), no. 2 (February 1993): 17. Based on the World Health Organization's Expanded Program for Immunization 1989 report published in Geneva.

27. "Rabies Threat at Southeast Border," *Helsingin Sanomat* (Helsinki), September 20, 1993, p. 6, translated in JPRS, *JPRS Report, Epidemiology,* JPRS-TEP-93-026, November 4, 1993, p. 39, and Paivi Repo, "Doctors Warn: Disease that Had Become Extinct in Finland Will Spread Again from Russia if Vaccinations Are Neglected," *Helsingin Sanomat* (Helsinki), October 1, 1993, p. 6, translated in JPRS, *JPRS Report, Epidemiology,* JPRS-TEP-93-026, November 4, 1993, p. 38.

28. Brad Knickerbocker, "Hopes of Ecological Bliss Elude the Fomer Soviet Bloc," *Christian Science Monitor,* March 16, 1994, p. 6.

29. United Nations International Children's Emergency Fund, UNICEF International Child Development Centre Regional Monitoring Report, *Public Policy and Social Conditions,* no. 1 (November 1993): 44.

30. Author's interview with Aleksey Yablokov, head of Interagency Ecological Security Committee of the Russian Federation Security Council, Washington, D.C., March 23, 1994.

CHAPTER 1

1. Sergey Ovsiyenko, "A Radioactive Belt Is Tightening around the Territory of Russia," *Rossiyskiye vesti,* March 5, 1993, p. 5, translated in Joint Publications Research Service, *JPRS Report, Environmental Issues,* JPRS-TEN-93-008, March 31, 1993, pp. 24–26.

2. Igor Tsarev, "Nuclear Plague: The Unique Plan of the Russian Scientists Could Threaten the World with a New Unprecedented Disaster," *Trud* (Moscow), September 17, 1993, p. 6, translated in JPRS, *JPRS Report, Environmental Issues*, JPRS-TEN-93-026, November 24, 1993, pp. 42–44.

3. Unattributed response to reader's letter, "Is Radioactive Waste Being Stored in Moscow?" *Izvestiya* (Moscow), June 15, 1994, p. 11, translated in Foreign Broadcast Information Service, *FBIS Daily Report, Central Eurasia*, FBIS-SOV-94-117, p. 28.

4. Radiostantsiya Ekho Moskvy (Moscow), June 14, 1994, translated in JPRS, *JPRS Report, Environmental Issues*, JPRS–TEN-94-017, June 30, 1994, p. 32.

5. Vorfolomeyev, "Ekolgisheskay bezopasnost' segodnya."

6. Ibid.

7. Interfax (Moscow), January 21, 1994, transcribed in JPRS, *JPRS Report, Environmental Issues*, JPRS-TEN-94-003, February 7, 1994, p. 36.

8. George Rodrigue, "Pollution Woes Plague Former Soviet States," Knight-Ridder News Service, August 25, 1993.

9. Hannes Gamillschegg, "USSR Successor States Simply Dump Nuclear Waste into Nature," *Frankfurter Rundschau*, October 14, 1993, p. 1, translated in FBIS, *FBIS Daily Report, Central Eurasia*, FBIS-SOV-93-200, October 19, 1993, p. 1.

10. Sergey Kozlov, "Kazakhstan's Nuclear Surprises: The Republic Is Turning into a Radioactive Dump," *Nezavisimaya gazeta* (Moscow), January 19, 1993, p. 1, translated in JPRS, *JPRS Report, Environmental Issues*, JPRS-TEN-93-004, March 8, 1993, pp. 65–66.

11. Radio Rossii (Moscow), January 5, 1993, translated in FBIS, *FBIS Daily Report, Central Eurasia*, FBIS-SOV-93-003, January 6, 1993, p. 43.

12. "Russians Plan Nuclear Explosions," *Foreign Report*, issued by the *Economist Newspaper Limited* (London) March 3, 1994, pp. 4–7.

13. Aleksey Portanskiy, "Weapons-Grade Uranium from Russia Will Go to Fuel U.S. Nuclear Electric Power Stations," *Izvestiya* (Moscow), February 26, 1993, p. 3, translated in FBIS, *FBIS Daily Report, Central Eurasia*, FBIS-SOV-93-038, March 1, 1993, pp. 9–10.

14. William J. Broad, "Russian Says Soviet Atom Arsenal Was Larger Than West Estimated," *New York Times*, September 26, 1993, section 1, pp. 1, 16. An additional source reports that there are 720 tons of highly enriched uranium in Russia, 480 tons of which are in actual weapons. See Jonathan Dean, "The Final Stage of Nuclear Arms Control," *Washington Quarterly* 17, no. 4 (autumn 1994): 37.

15. Michael R. Gordon, "U.S. Asks Russia for Data on Its Stocks of Nuclear Material," *New York Times*, May 5, 1994, p. A12.

16. Tsarev, "Nuclear Plague."

17. Ibid.

18. London Financial Times Environment Database, "Nuclear Matters," *Energy Economist* (London), April 1, 1992.

19. An additional source reports that there are 125 tons of weapons-grade

plutonium in Russia, 70.7 tons of which are in spent fuel. See Dean, "The Final Stage of Nuclear Arms Control," p. 37.

20. "Russia Planning to Stop Weapon-Grade Plutonium Production," Radio Free Europe/Radio Liberty A-wire, March 22, 1994.

21. Thomas W. Lippman, "Russia Set to Close 3 Reactors," *Washington Post*, March 17, 1994, pp. A1, A37.

22. "Russia Planning to Stop Weapon-Grade Plutonium Production."

23. Author's interview with Leonid Bolshov, director, Nuclear Safety Institute, Russian Academy of Sciences, Washington, D.C., April 27, 1994.

24. Alla Yaroshinskaya, *Chernobyl': Sovershenno sekretno* (Moscow: Drugiye Berega, 1992). See especially pp. 250–575. To be published in english by the University of Nebraska Press under the title of *Chernobyl: Top Secret*.

25. Alla Yaroshinskaya, "The Secret Office of the CPSU Central Committee on Chernobyl: The First Secret Documents Being Published Call Into Question the Future of Nuclear Power Engineering in Russia," *Izvestiya* (Moscow), April 17, 1993, pp. 1, 5, translated in JPRS, *JPRS Report, Environmental Issues*, JPRS-TEN-93-014, May 28, 1993, pp. 48–54.

26. See also Alexander Roman Sich, *The Chornobyl Accident Revisited: Source Term Analysis and Reconstruction of Events during the Active Phase*, doctoral thesis, Massachusetts Institute of Technology, January 1994, pp. 67–81 and 207–34.

27. Jean-Francois Augereau, "From Chernobyl to Tomsk," *Le Monde* (Paris), April 21, 1993, pp. 1, 13, translated in JPRS, *JPRS Report, Environmental Issues*, JPRS-TEN-93-014, May 28, 1993, pp. 19–21.

28. Georgiy Dolzhenko, "How Sound Is the Sarcophagus?" *Rabochaya tribuna* (Moscow), November 3, 1992, p. 2, translated in JPRS, *JPRS Report, Engineering & Equipment*, JPRS-UEQ-92-013, December 31, 1992, pp. 12–13.

29. Personal conversation with the author, April, 1993.

30. Augereau, "From Chernobyl to Tomsk."

31. Dolzhenko, "How Sound Is the Sarcophagus?"

32. Doyle McManus, "The New, Dangerous Dominoes" and "Unwanted Russian Warheads a Prize Waiting to Fall into Wrong Hands," *Los Angeles Times*, May 9, 1994, pp. A1, 5. The 30,000 warhead count represents a highly uncertain estimate the CIA gave to Congress in mid-1992. The estimate reportedly has a margin of error of 5,000 nuclear weapons.

33. McManus, "Unwanted Russian Warheads."

34. Ibid.

35. Seymour M. Hersh, "The Wild East," *Atlantic Monthly*, June 1994, pp. 68–69.

36. Sergei Shargorodsky, "Commandos Find Russian Nuclear Security Faults," Radio Free Europe/Radio Liberty B-Wire, February 23, 1994.

37. *Rossiyskiye vesti* (Moscow), January 19, 1993, cited by Stephen Foye, Radio Free Europe/Radio Liberty Research, January 21, 1993.

38. Andrey Vaganov, "Russian Gosatomnadzor Thwarted. Russian Federation Defense Ministry and Atomic Energy Ministry are Sabotaging Creation

of Federal Control System at Their Nuclear Facilities," *Nezavisimaya gazeta* (Moscow), April 30, 1993, p. 2, translated in JPRS, *JPRS Report. Environmental Issues*, JPRS-TEN-93-017, July 6, 1993, pp. 20–21.

39. Presidential Directive no. 224, Russian Federation, April 9, 1993.

40. Vaganov, "Russian Gosatomnadzor Thwarted."

41. Cited by Tariq Rauf, "Cleaning Up with a Bang," *Bulletin of the Atomic Scientists* no. 1 (January-February 1992): pp. 9, 47, quoting Russell Seitz from a *New York Times* article by William Broad (November 4, 1991).

42. McManus, "Unwanted Russian Warheads."

43. Michael R. Gordon, "Russian Aide Says Gangsters Try to Steal Atom Material," *New York Times*, May 26, 1994, p. A5.

44. R. Jeffrey Smith, "Freeh Warns of a New Russian Threat," *Washington Post*, May 26, 1994, pp. A1, 40.

45. Hersh, "The Wild East," p. 72.

46. Steve Coll, "Nuclear Goods Traded in Post-Soviet Bazaar," *Washington Post*, May 15, 1993, pp. A1, 18–46.

47. "Stolen Uranium Seized from Arzamas-16 Inhabitants," *Moskovskiye novosti* (Moscow), January 3, 1993, excerpted in BBC Monitoring, *Summary of World Broadcasts: Weekly Economic Report, Former USSR*, SU/W0263, January 8, 1993, p. A/21.

48. "Stolen Radioactive Caesium Believed Smuggled into Estonia," *Izvestiya* (Moscow), September 10, 1992, excerpted in BBC Monitoring, *Summary of World Broadcasts: Former USSR*, SU/1489, September 18, 1992, p. A2/2.

49. John-Thor Dahlburg, "Nuclear Material, Know-How Seep out of Former Soviet Union," *Los Angeles Times*, December 28, 1992.

50. "Russian Servicemen Sell Radioactive Materials—Estonian Security Police," Radio Free Europe/Radio Liberty, *Daily Report*, March 28, 1994, p. 8.

51. Jüri Liim, "Radioactive Goods from Tallinn," *Rahva Haal* (Tallinn), July 6, 1993, p. 2, translated in FBIS, *FBIS Report, Central Eurasia*, FBIS-USR-93-106, August 16, 1993, p. 50.

52. Andrey Ishchenko, "President Informed that Butcher and Plumber Are Trading Uranium," *Novaya yezhednevnaya gazeta* (Moscow), June 9, 1994, p. 1, translated in FBIS, *FBIS Daily Report, Central Eurasia*, FBIS-SOV-94-111, June 9, 1994, pp. 35–36.

53. Rick Atkinson, "Smuggled Plutonium Seized," *Washington Post*, July 19, 1994, p. A14.

54. Ferdinand Protzman, "Germany Reaffirming Russian Origin of Seized Plutonium," *New York Times*, July 21, 1994, p. A13. The author cites Leopold Schuster, the head of the organized crime division of Germany's Federal Criminal Office in Wiesbaden, as the source of the information.

55. Craig R. Whitney, "Germans Seize 3d Atom Sample, Smuggled by Plane from Russia," *New York Times*, August 14, 1994.

56. Steve Coll, "Stolen Plutonium Linked to Arms Labs," *Washington Post*, August 17, 1994, p. A24.

57. Bernard Gray, et al., "From Russia with Love," *Financial Times* (London), August 19, 1994, p. A11.

58. "Three Arrested in St. Petersburg," *New York Times*, August 19, 1994, p. A11.

59. Craig R. Whitney, "Germans Seize More Weapons Material," *New York Times*, August 17, 1994, p. A13.

60. "Uranium in Moscow," *Christian Science Monitor*, August 25, 1994, p. 20.

61. Smith, "Freeh Warns of a New Russian Threat."

62. Fred Hiatt, "Russia Lacks Means to Fight Crime, Intelligence Chief Warns," *Washington Post*, May 27, 1994, p. A34.

63. Kirill Belyaninov, "The Players in This Shell Game Need Plutonium, Lead and Moxie," *New York Times*, February 27, 1994, section 1, p. 7. According to Hersh's article, "The Wild East," p. 74, Belyaninov and his colleagues were also shown a warhead from a Soviet SS-20 nuclear missile and told that it was for sale for $70,000.

CHAPTER 2

1. Bronwen Maddox, "A Fall-out among Friends," *Financial Times* (London), November 16, 1993, p. 16.

2. Kjell Dragnes, "Wild Growth in the Wake of the Accident," *Aftenposten* (Oslo), November 16, 1993, p. 13, translated in Foreign Broadcast Information Service, *FBIS Report, Central Eurasia*, FBIS-USR-93-160, December 16, 993, pp. 1–2. Also see London Financial Times Environment Database, "Nuclear Matters," *Energy Economist* (London), April 1, 1992.

3. London Financial Times Environment Database, "Nuclear Matters."

4. Chrystia Freeland, "Waiting for the Next Chernobyl," *Financial Times* (London), April 21, 1993, p. 20.

5. Sich, *The Chornobyl Accident Revisited*, p. 127.

6. Mike Edwards, "Living with the Monster Chornobyl," *National Geographic*, August 1994, pp. 100–115. The photographs that accompany the two articles on pollution and Chernobyl provide perhaps the most graphic visual evidence of the ecological catastrophe that has taken place within the FSU.

7. Dragnes, "Wild Growth in the Wake of the Accident," p. 1.

8. Professor Y. Petryayev, cited in O. Yegorova, "Is One Chernobyl Not Enough for Us?" *Komsomol'skaya pravda* (Moscow), November 19, 1992, p. 2, translated in Joint Publications Research Service (hereafter "JPRS"), *JPRS Report, Engineering & Equipment, Central Eurasia*, JPRS-UEQ-92-013, December 31, 1992, pp. 20–21.

9. A. A. Ivanov, "A Clinical-Population Analysis of the Immune System Response of Workers at the Chernobyl AES and the Population of the Surrounding Territories," *Meditsinskaya radiologiya* (Moscow), vol. 38, no. 2

(February 1993): 24–28, translated in JPRS, *JPRS Report, Science and Technology, Life Sciences,* JPRS-ULS-93-011, October 7, 1993, p. 26.

10. Ibid.

11. Dragnes, "Wild Growth in the Wake of the Accident."

12. Ibid. Also see the French Nuclear Safty Institute's study of 2,651 children in Ukraine cited in *CIS Environmental Watch* no. 6, published by the Center for Russian and Eurasian Studies, Monterey Institute of International Studies, Monterey, Calif., spring 1994, p. 76, showing a rate of 100 cases per 100,000 instead of the normal rate of 0.1 to 0.3 cases per 100,000 people that year.

13. Edwards, "Living with the Monster Chornobyl." Morris Rosen, the deputy director of the Nuclear Safety Division of the International Atomic Energy Agency (in Vienna), "was surprised by and skeptical of Sich's conclusion that virtually all the material dumped . . . missed the core entirely. . . . [To Rosen] It's a new theory that I haven't heard of, but I can't say it's crazy." These citations are from David L. Chandler, in his *Boston Globe* article of January 30, 1994, entitled "Study Says Chernobyl Core Melted Down: MIT Researcher Finds Radioactivity Far Worse than Soviets Reported." Rosen's current evaluation of the Sich thesis regarding the failure of the Soviet helicopters to cover the core with sand and other materials, is not known. Sich persists in asserting that "significantly more radioactivity was released because the core was not covered during the approximately ten-day period of the Active Phase of the accident." From the errata sheets signed by Sich on July 21, 1994.

14. Sich, *The Chornobyl Accident Revisited,* p. 73. For an excellent summary of Sich's work, see David L. Chandler, "Chernobyl: What Really Went on During Those 10 Harrowing Days," *Boston Globe,* January 31, 1994, p. 25. Sich's estimates of radioactivity and consequent danger to the population—as high as they are in comparison with the original Soviet estimates—may even be an understatement. Alexander Bolsunovsky in his article "Assessing Chernobyl Transuranium Element Releases," *CIS Environmental Watch,* no. 6, Center for Russian and Eurasian Studies, Monterey Institute of International Studies, Monterey, Calif., spring 1994, pp. 6–25, observed that Sich failed to adequately consider transuranium elements. See especially endnote 61, p. 25.

15. Sich, *The Chornobyl Accident Revisited,* p. 392. Sich has amended his dissertation to account for a "serious error" in the "initial core inventory of yield of Cs-136: (from the errata sheets received on October 4, 1994 from the Department of Nuclear Engineering, Massachusetts Institute of Technology, Cambridge, Massachusetts). As a result of his recalculations, he finds that "as a rough estimate, the release value is approximately 120 ± 50 MCi for the three volatile elements iodine, cesium, and tellurium. This still contrasts significantly with the Soviet *total* release value of 50 MCi (which includes the three elements considered in the table plus others) . . . albeit biased toward a lower release . . . the *total* activity . . . as a result of the Chornobyl accident was approximately 150 ± 50 MCi—more than three times that reported by the Soviets." While not four to five times greater, as in his original estimates, the revised estimate is still significantly higher than official figures.

16. Alan Weisman, "Journey through a Doomed Land: Exploring Chernobyl's Still-Deadly Ruins," *Harper's*, August 1994, pp. 45–53.

17. Interview with Mykhaylo Kuzmenko, chief of the Freshwater Radioecology Department, Ukranian Hydrobiology Institute, by Mykhaylo Prylutskyy, "What Kind of Water Is the Donbass Drinking?" *Zelenyy Svit* (Moscow), no. 8 (June 1994): 4, translated in FBIS, *FBIS Daily Report, Central Eurasia*, FBIS-SOV-94-131, July 11, 1994, pp. 76–78.

18. Ibid.

19. Sich, *The Chornobyl Accident Revisited*, p. 67. Also see the official document on the Chernobyl accident: "Memorandum to Acting Prime Minister of Ukraine Yukhym Zvyagilskyy: Minpryrody (Ministry of Environmental Protection) of Ukraine Position Regarding Possibility of Continuing Operation of Chernobyl AES," *Ukrayinska gazeta* (Kiev), no. 18 (November 4–17, 1993): 4, translated in JPRS, *JPRS Report, Science and Technology, Science and Technology Policy*, JPRS-UST-94-005, February 10, 1994, pp. 27–28.

20. Hans A. Bethe, "Chernobyl: It Can't Happen Here," *New York Times*, May 2, 1991, p. A25.

21. Sich, *The Chornobyl Accident Revisited*, pp. 227–28.

22. Ibid, p. 145. Also see Grigorii Medvedev, *The Truth about Chernobyl*, trans. Evelyn Rossiter (New York: Basic Books, 1991) which contains a foreword by Andrei Sakharov; and Zhores A. Medvedev, *The Legacy of Chernobyl*, 1st ed. (New York: W. W. Norton, 1990).

23. Sich, *The Chornobyl Accident Revisited*, p. 159

24. Ibid.

25. Ibid, pp. 156–61.

26. Murray Feshbach, "Civilian Nuclear Reactors in the Former USSR: Desperation and Danger," unpublished research paper, Georgetown University, 1993.

27. Sich, *The Chornobyl Accident Revisited*, p. 415.

28. Ibid.

29. Vlad Ignatov and Vera Romanova, "Russia's Nuclear Facilities Inventoried: Absolutely No Order," *Segodnya* (Moscow), February 1994, translated in JPRS, *JPRS Report, Science & Technology*, JPRS-UST-94-008, March 31, 1994.

30. Erik Solem, *Strategic Nuclear Materials Safeguards and Reactor Safety in the Commonwealth of Independent States and Eastern Europe*, project report no. PR 615, Operational Research and Analysis Establishment, Directorate of Social and Economic Analysis, Department of National Defence, Ottawa, Canada, December 1992, pp 21–22.

31. Solem, *Strategic Nuclear Materials Safeguards*, p. 16. The VVER-440 model V230 was the first commercially viable civilian-use reactor to be installed in the Soviet Union. There were two earlier prototypes (VVER-210 and VVER-365) developed in the late 1950s and constructed at the Novoronezh AES. Although these two prototypes were incapable of providing great amounts of power (such as produced by the RBMKs), they were only shut down in 1984 and 1990, respectively.

32. Ignatov and Romanova, "Russia's Nuclear Facilities Inventoried"; and Feshbach, "Civilian Nuclear Reactors in the Former USSR," pp. 3–7.

33. Rudolf Eickeler, "Danilov-Danilyan: Chernobyl-type Reactors Cannot Be Improved with Western Technology," *Handelsblatt* (Duesseldorf), November 1, 1993, p. 12, translated in JPRS, *JPRS Report, Environmental Issues,* JPRS-TEN-93-027, December 15, 1993, pp. 42–43.

34. Eickeler, "Danilov-Danilyan."

35. Erik Solem, *Strategic Nuclear Materials Safeguards,* p. 17.

36. Thomas W. Lippman, "Ukraine Moves to Shut Chernobyl Plant," *Washington Post,* April 10, 1994, p. A 22.

37. Euroscope Database (Brussels), "Nuclear: Liberal MEPS Debate Safety in CIS and Eastern Europe," May 9, 1992, transcribed in JPRS, *JPRS Report, Environmental Issues,* JPRS-TEN-92-004-L, September 14, 1992, p. 59.

38. Ignatov and Romanova, "Russia's Nuclear Facilities Inventoried"; and Feshbach, "Civilian Nuclear Reactors in the Former USSR," pp. 3-7.

39. Solem, *Strategic Nuclear Materials Safeguards,* pp. 17–21.

40. Sich, *The Chornobyl Accident Revisited,* p. 67.

41. Ibid., pp. 21–24.

42. Memos by V. Gubarev, editor, Science Department, *Pravda,* and V. Shcherbitskiy, first secretary of the Central Committee of the Communist Party of Ukraine, *Visnyk akademiyi nauk Ukrayiny* (Kiev), no. 9 (September, 1992): 95–98, translated in JPRS, *JPRS Report, Engineering & Equipment, Central Eurasia,* JPRS-UEQ-92-013, December 31, 1992, pp. 9–12.

43. Sich, *The Chornobyl Accident Revisited,* p. 24.

44. Richard Boudreaux, "Russian Panel Finds Crisis in Nuclear-Power Safety," *Los Angeles Times,* February 16, 1994, p. A 2. See also ITAR-TASS World Service (Moscow), February 15, 1994, transcribed in BBC Monitoring, *Summary of World Broadcasts: Weekly Economic Report, Former USSR,* SWU/0322, March 4, 1994, p. WE/1.

45. Bodreaux, "Russian Panel Finds Crisis in Nuclear-Power Safety."

46. Ignatov and Romanova, "Russia's Nuclear Facilities Inventoried."

47. Vladimir Kuznetsov, "The Territory of the Former Soviet Union Presents Greater Radiation Danger than Ever—And There Is More than Enough Evidence of It," *Segodnya* (Moscow), no. 56 (September 23, 1993): 6, translated in JPRS, *JPRS Report, Environmental Issues,* JPRS-TEN-93-026, November 24, 1993, pp. 52–55.

48. BBC Monitoring, *Summary of World Broadcasts: Weekly Economic Report, Former USSR,* SU/W0250, October 2, 1992, p. A/11.

49. Sveriges Radio Network (Stockholm), March 26, 1992, translated in FBIS, *FBIS Daily Report, Central Eurasia,* FBIS-SOV-92-060, March 27, 1992, p. 2; and K. Belyaninov, "Leningrad Nuclear Power Station Accident: It Could Have Been Worse," *Komsomol'skaya pravda* (Moscow), April 4, 1992, p. 2, translated in JPRS, *JPRS Report, Environmental Issues,* JPRS-TEN-92-009, May 22, 1992, p. 65.

50. Postfactum news service (Moscow), April 30, 1992, transcribed in FBIS, *FBIS Daily Report, Central Eurasia,* FBIS-SOV-92-085, May 1, 1992, p. 33.

51. Anatoliy Kuznetsov, ITAR-TASS (Moscow), May 29, 1992, transcribed in FBIS, *FBIS Daily Report, Central Eurasia,* FBIS-SOV-92-106, June 2, 1992, p. 26.

52. State Committee for Atomic Supervision (Russian Federation), "Safety Regulations Violated," *Holos Ukrayiny* (Kiev), September 26, 1992, p. 1, translated in FBIS, *FBIS Daily Report, Central Eurasia,* FBIS-SOV-92-191, October 1, 1992, p. 36.

53. Veronika Romanenkova, "Condensate Tank Leak at Kola Nuke Station Posed No Hazard," ITAR-TASS (Moscow), September 15, 1992, transcribed in JPRS, *JPRS Report, Environmental Issues,* JPRS-TEN-92-019, October 7, 1992, p. 52.

54. "Kozloduy Incident Was 'Serious,'" Radio Free Europe/Radio Liberty, *Daily Report,* no. 18, January 28, 1993.

55. Radio Vilnius Network, October 15, 1992, translated in FBIS, *FBIS Daily Report, Central Eurasia,* FBIS-SOV-92-200, October 15, 1992, pp. 59–60.

56. Interfax (Moscow), "A Minor Incident at the Kursk Atomic Power Station," December 31, 1992

57. Chrystia Freeland, "Chernobyl Fires Revive Fears of Ukrainian Reactors' Safety," *Financial Times,* January 15, 1993, p. A28.

58. Ukrinform (Kiev), April 29, 1993, translated in BBC Monitoring, *Summary of World Broadcasts: Weekly Economic Report, Central Eurasia,* SU/W0280, May 7, 1993, p. A/13.

59. Agence France Presse (Paris), November 24, 1993, transcribed in FBIS, *FBIS Daily Report, Central Eurasia,* FBIS-SOV-93-225, November 24, 1993, p. 42.

60. "Nuclear Plant's Reactor Shut Down after Leak," Radio Free Europe/Radio Liberty A-Wire, February 22, 1994.

61. "Fire Latest Incident in Ukraine Nuclear Power Network," Radio Free Europe/Radio Liberty B-wire, March 17, 1994.

62. Matthew J. Sagers, "The Energy Industries of the Former USSR: A Mid-Year Survey," *Post-Soviet Geography* 34, no. 6 (1993): 341–418. Using 1900 rubles per U.S. dollar (the early 1994 rate of exchange), these numbers translate into about $980 million and $600 million, respectively.

63. Interfax (Moscow), July 1, 1994, transcribed in FBIS, *FBIS Daily Report, Central Eurasia,* FBIS-SOV-94-128, July 5, 1994, p. 28.

64. "Halting AES Is Not Like Closing a Barn," *Rossiyskaya gazeta* (Moscow), February 10, 1994, p. 1, translated in FBIS, *FBIS Daily Report, Central Eurasia,* FBIS-SOV-94-028, February 10, 1994, p. 38. Also see Radio Free Europe/Radio Liberty A-wire, Moscow, April 8, 1994. The report cites Atomic Energy Minister Mikhaylov's figure of 450 billion rubles, or $250 million, owed to the nuclear industry. Also see Interfax (Moscow), July 1, 1994, transcribed in FBIS, *FBIS Daily Report, Central Eurasia,* FBIS-SOV-94-128, July 5, 1994, p. 28.

65. Interfax (Moscow), July 1, 1994, transcribed in FBIS, *FBIS Daily Report, Central Eurasia,* FBIS-SOV-94-128, July 5, 1994, p. 28.

66. Interfax (Moscow), February 20, 1994, transcribed in FBIS, *FBIS Daily Report, Central Eurasia,* FBIS-SOV-94-035, February 22, 1994, p. 38.

67. Ibid.

68. Interfax (Moscow), February 22, 1994, transcribed in FBIS, *FBIS Daily Report, Central Eurasia,* FBIS-SOV-94-035, February 22, 1994, pp. 38–39.

69. Ibid.

70. Radio Rossii (Moscow), April 2, 1993, translated in BBC Monitoring, *Summary of World Broadcasts: Weekly Economic Report, Former USSR,* SU/WO276, April 9, 1993, p. A/15.

71. Ustina Markus, "International Atomic Energy Agency to Hold Session on Chornobyl," Radio Free Europe/Radio Liberty, *Daily Report,* no. 76, April 21, 1994, p. 6.

72. Yuriy Bersenev, "The Country's Nuclear Weapons Complex Is in Pitiful Condition: The Equipment Is Aging Physically and the People Are Working at the Limit of What Is Feasible," *Nezavisimaya gazeta* (Moscow), June 28, 1994, p. 6, translated in JPRS, *JPRS Report, Military Affairs,* JPRS-UMA-94-029, July 8, 1994, p. 18.

73. Viktor Demidenko and Mikhail Melnik, ITAR-TASS (Moscow), May 16, 1994, transcribed in FBIS, *FBIS Daily Report, Central Eurasia,* FBIS-SOV-94-094, May 16, 1994, p. 44. Ivan Selin, head of the U.S. Nuclear Regulatory Commission, estimates $20 billion is required.

CHAPTER 3

1. Wayne C. Hanson, "Radioactive Contamination in Arctic Tundra Ecosystems," paper prepared for the Interagency Arctic Research Policy Committee, Workshop on Arctic Contamination, Anchorage, May 2–7, 1993. The story of the irradiated migratory ducks was related to the author by a faculty member at the University of Connecticut in Storrs. While I have not confirmed this specific report, I have heard similar tales of irradiated migratory birds in Latin America but do not know if they originated in Alaska as well.

2. Thomas Cochran et al., *Soviet Nuclear Weapons: Nuclear Weapons Handbook* vol. IV (New York: Harper and Row, 1989), p. 373.

3. Ibid. Alternatively, 115 "peaceful" explosions have been reported. More importantly, Mikhaylov stated that 30 percent of these vented. In addition, oil domes and diamond fields opened up by these explosions remain radioactive.

4. Ibid. See also Frederic Hauge, "Environmental Problems in Northern Russia: Causes, Consequences and Solutions," unpublished paper, Bellona Foundation in cooperation with the Komsomolets Foundation, 193, p. 5.

5. Hauge, "Environmental Problems in Northern Russia."

6. Geoffrey Lean, "Yeltsin Learns Full Scale of Horror," *Observer* (London), April 11, 1993.

7. Ibid. Also see Arkadiy Dubnov, "Aleksey Yablokov: 'The Threat of Ecological Disaster Is No Secret to the President,'" *New Times* (Moscow), no. 14

(April 1992): pp. 11–13, transcribed in Foreign Broadcast Information Service, *FBIS Daily Report, Central Eurasia,* FBIS-SOV-92-090, May 8, 1992.

8. Igor D. Spassky, "Apathy Above, Terror Below," *New York Times,* June 3, 1993, p. A 23.

9. ITAR-TASS (Moscow), November 25, 1992, transcribed in Joint Publications Research Service, *JPRS Report, Environmental Issues,* JPRS-TEN-92-023, December 30, 1992, p. 55.

10. Vladimir Borovkov, Murmansk Fisheries and Oceanography Institute, at the Rubin International Symposium "On the Discussion of Results of 1993 Expedition to SSN Komsomolets and on the Working Out of a Common Concept for Further Research," January 31–February 2, 1994, St. Petersburg.

11. Author's interview with Kathleen Crane, Washington, D.C., May 2, 1994.

12. ITAR-TASS (Moscow), July 14, 1994, transcribed in FBIS, *FBIS Daily Report, Central Eurasia,* FBIS-SOV-94-136, July 15, 1994, p. 23; and Radio Moscow, August 1, 1994, transcribed in FBIS, *FBIS Daily Report, Central Eurasia,* FBIS-SOV-94-147, August 1, 1994, p. 20.

13. Thomas Nilsen and Nils Bøhmer, *Sources to Radioactive Contamination in Murmansk and Arkhangel'sk Counties,* Bellona Report, vol. 1, (Oslo: Bellona Foundation,1994), p. 12. The Bellona Report was funded in part by the Norwegian government. According to a statement by John Sprange of Greenpeace in 1993, in all of Russia there were 228 nuclear submarines with 394 reactors and 7 nuclear icebreakers with 13 reactors. Sprange was cited by Edith M. Lederer, "Russia Can't Guarantee Safety of Nuclear Submarines," Associated Press, March 30, 1993. I have heard other reports suggesting that 100 of the nuclear submarine reactors have been removed from "active service."

14. More than twenty thousand used nuclear fuel rods are stored on the Kola Peninsula. Frederic Hauge of the Bellona Foundation in Oslo described bases as having "improvised, essentially sub-standard storage facilities" characterized by the Yablokov Commission report as needing "urgent" improvement in the storage arrangements for these waste materials. See Hauge, "Environmental Problems in Northern Russia," p. 4.

15. Vlad Ignatov and Vera Romanova, "Russia's Nuclear Facilities Inventoried: Absolutely No Order," *Segodnya,* no. 24 (February 1994): 9, translated in JPRS, *JPRS Report, Science & Technology,* JPRS-UST-94-008, March 31, 1994, p. 48. The most complete official report on the problem of nuclear waste being created by the Russian Northern Fleet is the "Report of Russia's Ministry of Protection of the Environment and Natural Resources on an Urgent Solution to the Problem of Handling Liquid Radioactive Waste from Transport-Type Nuclear Power Plants and Creating a System of Radio-Environmental Monitoring in the Waters of the Russian Federation," developed by the Interagency Working Group on Problems of Handling Liquid Radioactive Waste, headed by V. V. Kutsenko, December 15, 1993.

16. Igor Tsarev, "Nuclear Plague: The Unique Plan of the Russian Scientists Could Threaten the World with a New Unprecedented Disaster," *Trud*

(Moscow), September 17, 1993, p. 6, translated in JPRS, *JPRS Report, Environmental Issues,* JPRS-TEN-93-026, November 24, 1993, pp. 42–44.

17. H. Tjonn, "Russians to Build Nuclear Waste Dump," *Aftenposten* (Oslo), June 4, 1993, p. 12, translated in JPRS, *JPRS Environmental Issues,* JPRS-TEN-93-018, July 9, 1993, p. 29.

18. Lederer, "Russia Can't Guarantee Safety of Nuclear Submarines."

19. See Bill Powell and Genine Babakian, "Nuclear Waste: Russia's Secret Dumping Ground," *Newsweek,* November 1, 1993.

20. Joshua Handler, "Soviet Subs—a Neglected Nuclear Time Bomb," *Christian Science Monitor,* December 18, 1991, p. 19.

21. Frederic Hauge, "Environmental Problems in Northern Russia," p. 4.

22. Nilsen and Bøhmer, *Sources to Radioactive Contamination in Murmansk and Arkhangel'sk Counties,* cited by Marat Zubko, "Unknown Accident at Northern Fleet Radioactive Waste Storage Facility," *Izvestiya,* April 1, 1993, p. 6, translated in JPRS, *JPRS Report, Environmental Issues,* JPRS-TEN-93-011, April 27, 1993, pp. 24–25.

23. Ibid. Not mentioned in this list is the Russian submarine that was hit by the *U.S.S. Grayling* in the Barents Sea in March 1993.

24. Roman Zadunaiskiy, ITAR-TASS (Moscow), January 21, 1993, transcribed in FBIS, *FBIS Daily Report, Central Eurasia,* FBIS-SOV-93-013, January 22, 1993, p. 40.

25. Letter to the author from Joshua Handler dated April 1, 1994.

26. Joshua Handler, "Russia's Pacific Fleet: Submarine Bases and Facilities," *Jane's Intelligence Review,* no. 4 (April 1994): 166–171, especially p. 166.

27. Lyudmila Zhukova, "We All Live off a Yellow Submarine," *Moscow News,* no. 28, July 12, 1992, p. 11, transcribed in JPRS, *JPRS Report, Engineering & Equipment, Central Eurasia,* JPRS-UEQ-92-011, October 6, 1992, p. 9.

28. Dubnov, "Aleksey Yablokov: 'The Threat of Ecological Disaster.'"

29. U.S. Congress, Senate, statement of Robert N. Gates, director of Central Intelligence, "Radioactive and Other Environmental Threats to the United States and the Arctic Resulting from Past Soviet Activities," hearing before the Select Committee on Intelligence 102d Congress, 2d Sess., August 15, 1992, pp. 122–38.

30. Cited by Yereth Rosen, "USSR Leaves Radioactive Legacy," *Christian Science Monitor,* August 26, 1992, p. 8.

31. Hal Bernton, "Russian Revelations Indicate Arctic Region Is Awash in Contaminants," *Washington Post,* May 17, 1993, p. A3. The article is a brief summary of the International Workshop on Arctic Contamination, Anchorage, Alaska, May 2–7, 1993.

32. Kathleen Crane and Stephanie Pfirman, "Regional Dispersal of Contaminants in the Arctic," paper prepared for the Interagency Arctic Research Policy Committee, Workshop on Arctic Contamination, Anchorage, Alaska, May 2–7, 1993. Much of the data in this report was drawn from an Arctic Environmental Atlas being produced by the Environmental Defense Fund. The workshop papers were assembled under the direction of Bruce F. Molnia, United States Geological Survey.

33. Interfax (Moscow), April 16, 1993 (in English).

34. Although known and discussed previously in various sources, for example in the 1979 and 1983 yearbooks of the Stockholm International Peace Research Institute (SIPRI), the impact on the consciousness of the world seems to have been minimal overall. Even discussions at Geneva by the United Nations under the leadership of the Swedish government did not result in major resolutions to mitigate the potential hazards of these chemical weapon dumpings.

35. Phillip Knightley, "Dumps of Death," *Sunday Times Magazine* (London), April 5, 1992, pp. 26–30.

36. Svetlana Stepunina, "Vladimir Karasev, Responsible Secretary of the Russian Federation President's Council for Ecological Policy: 'And the Committee for Emergency Situations Will Become the Country's Leading Ministry . . . ,'" *Rossiyskiye vesti* (Moscow), June 4, 1993, pp. 3–4, translated in FBIS, *FBIS Daily Report, Central Eurasia,* FBIS-USR-93-076, June 21, 1993, pp. 38–41.

37. Also Radio Vilnius Network, June 26, 1992, translated in FBIS, *FBIS Daily Report, Central Eurasia,* FBIS-SOV-92-126, July 1992, p. 9; and *Rossiyskaya gazeta* (Moscow), July 22, 1992, p. 7.

38. I. Rudnikov, "Where Are the Wehrmacht's Chemical Munitions?" *Komsomol'skaya pravda* (Moscow), July 16, 1992, p. 2, translated in FBIS, *FBIS Daily Report, Central Eurasia,* FBIS-SOV-92-138, (July 17, 1992), p. 7.

39. Author's interview with Alexey Yablokov.

40. London Financial Times Environment Database, "Nuclear Matters," *Energy Economist* (London) April 1, 1992. Discussions about this site were conducted by the author in Estonia in February 1994 at a U.S. Institute of Peace-sponsored conference on conflict resolution related to ethnic issues and environmental hazards.

41. Raimo Mustonen, "Sillamäe Is Not Chernobyl. The Investigative Commission's Interim Report on Sillamäe Is Ready," *Rahva Haal* (Tallinn), May 7, 1993, translated by Rein Sikk, Helsinki. I am indebted to Lya Karm, Baltic Foundation, Washington, D.C., for providing me with a copy of this translation.

42. *Daily Telegraph,* September 2, 1992; and *Helsingen Sanomat* (Helsinki), September 4, 1992, p. 20.

43. This very different figure was cited by a Russian participant from Sillamäe at the conflict resolution discussions conducted in Tallinn, noted above.

CHAPTER *4*

1. Goskompriroda SSSR (State Committee on Nature Protection), *Gosudarstvenniy doklad: Sostoyanie prirodnoy sredy i prirordookhrannaya deyatelnost' v SSSR v 1989 godu* (Moscow, Youth Institute of the Komsomol and Goskomtrud, 1990), p. 94, and Table 18, p. 99.

2. N. Glukhoyedov and L. Oganesyan, "The Mineral-Raw Material Base and Geological Service of the Russian Federation," *Segodnya* (Moscow), May 31, 1994, p. 13, translated in Foreign Broadcast Information Service, *FBIS Daily Report, Central Eurasia,* FBIS-USR-94-067, June 23, 1994, pp. 1–2. The authors indicate that among the largest cities that currently utilize such surface water unprotected from pollution are Moscow, St. Petersburg, Vologda, Kostroma, Kirov, Astrakhan, Kurgan, Chelyabinsk, Perm, and Omsk.

3. AID/EPA work on the Moscow area water problem, however, is an important project currently being carried out. Another project on the Volga basin in cooperation with the Canadians has begun as well.

4. D. J. Peterson, "The State of the Environment: The Water," Radio Free Europe/Radio Liberty, *Report on the USSR,* March 16, 1990, p. 14–19.

5. Ministerstvo prirodopol'zovaniya i okhrany okruzhayushchey sredy SSSR (Ministry of Nature Utilization and Safeguarding of the Environment of the USSR), "Natsional'nyy doklad SSSR k konferentsii OON 1992 goda po okruzhayushchey srede i razvitiyu," draft document prepared for the Rio Summit, Moscow, 1991, p. 181.

6. Leyla Boulton, "Leyla Boulton Samples Russia's Contaminated Supplies," *Financial Times* (London), April 7, 1993.

7. *Izvestiya* (Moscow), October 8, 1992, translated in BBC Monitoring, *Summary of World Broadcasts, Weekly Economic Report, Former USSR,* SU/W0253, October 23, 1992, p. A/13.

8. "Inspectors Find Purification Facilities in Moscow Unsafe," Radio Free Europe/Radio Liberty, *Daily Report,* March 17, 1994.

9. Vorfolomeyev, "Ekologicheskaya bezopasnost' segodnya," *Zelenyy mir* (Moscow) no. 3, (February 1, 1993): 4.

10. Alvin Rubenstein and Igor Zonn, "Tragedy in the Aral Sea Basin: Looking Back to Plan Ahead?" paper presented at a Villanova University seminar, "Central Asia: Its Strategic Importance and Future Prospects," Villanova, Pa., October 20–30, 1992, p. 15.

11. Ibid.

12. Known in classical times as the Oxus and Jaxartes rivers, respectively.

13. S. Zalygin, et al., "Voda v setyakh Minvodkhoza," *Izvestiya* (Moscow), February 7, 1990; and Murray Feshbach, "The Urals, Kazakhstan and the Aral Sea: One Worse than the Other," *Japan Energy Review,* no. 3 (February 1994): 6–13.

14. Diversification of land use for planting of money crops, which require less water than utilized for the cotton monoculture of the region, should be implemented in order to reduce the extremely high demand for water.

15. A major research study is being conducted by Wellstart International on the issue of breast milk contamination in Central Asia. This research, under the sponsorship of the U.S. Agency for International Development, is designed to provide a scientific study of the alleged problem. Their work should yield a more scientific, transparent analysis of the extent of the problem. Most importantly, it will determine if the problem actually exists to the extent that Soviet

literature reported. Among others, see Sally Ann Lederman, "Environmental Contaminants and Their Significance for Breastfeeding in the Central Asian Republics," Wellstart, Washington, D.C., July 1993.

16. S. K. Kamalov, *Sudba Arala-Sudba Narodov,* presented at the ISAR (formerly the Institute for Soviet American Relations) forum, Almaty, fall 1992, pp. 15–16.

17. Agence France Press (Paris), October 17, 1992, transcribed in Joint Publications Research Service, *JPRS Report, Environmental Issues,* JPRS-TEN-92-021, November 12, 1992, p. 1.

18. I am indebted to Keith Bush, formerly of Radio Free Europe/Radio Liberty for this source.

19. John Pomfret, "Black Sea, Strangled by Pollution, Is Near Ecological Death," *Washington Post,* June 20, 1994, pp. A1, 10.

20. Agence France Presse (Paris), October 17, 1992, transcribed in JPRS, *JPRS Report, Environmental Issues,* November 12, 1992, p. 1.

21. Vladimir Novak, ITAR-TASS (Moscow), April 7, 1993, transcribed in JPRS, *JPRS Report, Environmental Issues,* JPRS-TEN-93-010, April 20, 1993, p. 21. The measure to prohibit the dumping of radioactive materials into the Black Sea is almost unique. Only one reference has been found to indicate that radioactive materials were dumped into this sea.

22. V. Loukjanenko, "Water Crisis in the USSR," *World Health* (January-February 1990): pp. 132–33.

23. Ministry of Nature Utilization and Safeguarding of the Environment of the USSR, *Natsional'nyy doklad,* p. 187.

24. ITAR-TASS (Moscow), February 9, 1994, transcribed in BBC Monitoring, *Summary of World Broadcasts, Weekly Economic Report, Former USSR,* SU/W0322, March 4, 1994, p. WE/1.

25. K. Amenniyazov, cited by V. Kuleshov, "Turkmenistan Insists on Joint Action to Protect against the Approach of the Caspian," *Izvestiya,* April 6, 1993, p. 4, translated in JPRS, *JPRS Report, Environmental Issues,* JPRS-TEN-93-011, April 27, 1993, pp. 41–42.

26. "Their Dollars for Our Environment," *Rossiyskaya gazeta* (Moscow), June 10, 1994, p. 3, translated in JPRS, *JPRS Report, Environmental Issues,* JPRS-TEN-94-017, June 30, 1994, p. 33–34. The work of George Davis in this region under the sponsorship of AID is particularly important.

27. "Another Russian Horror Story," *Foreign Report,* no. 2263, issued by the *Economist Newspaper Limited* (London), July 17, 1993, p. 4.

28. Cited in Raymond Bonner, "Wars Envelop Armenia, Corroding Environment," *New York Times,* August 17, 1993, p. A2.

29. See interview by Ludmilla Sorokina with Yury Novikov and Sofiya Plitman, Russian Academy of Medical Sciences, "What Is Flowing into the 'Little Spring,'" *Rossiyskiye vesti* (Moscow), June 11, 1993, p. 4.

30. This section is far from a complete examination of all severely polluted bodies of water in the FSU. Cleaning up all the polluted waters will require much more corrective action than has been taken up to this point.

CHAPTER 5

1. James Adams, "The Red Death: The Untold Story of Russia's Secret Biological Weapons," *Sunday Times* (London), March 27, 1994, section 4, pp. 1–2. See also James Adams, *The New Spies: Exploring the Frontiers of Espionage* (London: Hutchinson, 1994), pp. 270–83.

2. Adams, "The Red Death."

3. Ibid.

4. Ibid.

5. Interview with Vil Mirzayanov by Konstantin Katanyan, "They Wanted to Make Me the Scapegoat," *Kuranty* (Moscow), January 23, 1993, p. 5, translated in Joint Publication Research Service, *JPRS Report, Environmental Issues,* JPRS-TEN-93-004, March 8, 1993, p. 40. There continues to be considerable disagreement among Russian officials as to the exact number of chemical weapons stored in Russia. Victor Goslov, deputy chief of the Directorate of Ecology Safety of the Ministry of Environmental Protection and Natural Resources, restated in February 1994 the government claim that it possessed 40,000 tons of chemical weapons in seven depots. He also stated that the government was "studying" the demand for setting up mobile plants to liquidate the chemical weapons. Mayak Radio Network (Moscow), February 15, 1994, transcribed in BBC Monitoring, *Summary of World Broadcasts, Former USSR,* SU/1925, February 18, 1994, p. 91. Yablokov told a conference at George Mason University on March 16, 1994 that he had considerable doubt about the 40,000 figure and suspected that the real figure could be ten times greater, stored in some three hundred separate locations. The seven special-purpose arsenals where the Russians admit to storing at least 40,000 tons chemical weapons are located at the settlement of Gornyy (Saratov oblast), the city of Kambarka and the settlement of Kizner (Udmurtia), the city of Shchuchye (Kurgan oblast), the city of Pochep (Bryansk oblast), the settlement of Leonilovka (Penza oblast), and the settlement of Maradykovkiy (Kirov oblast), according to Igor Vlasov, "Chemical 'Thorns' in the Country's Side," *Rossiyskaya gazeta* (Moscow), January 15, 1994, p. 3, translated in JPRS, *JPRS Report, Environmental Issues,* JPRS-TEN-94-003, February 7, 1994, pp. 34–35.

6. Richard Boudreaux, "Yeltsin Fires Official in Charge of Destroying Russia's Chemical Arms," *Los Angeles Times,* April 8, 1994, p. A4; and R. Jeffrey Smith, "U.S. Believes Russians Still Work on Bio Weapons," *Washington Post,* April 8, 1994, p.1.

7. Valentina Morozova and Dmitriy Kuybyshev, "Chemical Arms Problems in Bryansk Area. Chemical Bombs May Sleep Tight," *Kommersant-Daily,* (Moscow), July 2, 1994, p. 21, translated in Foreign Broadcast Information Service, *FBIS Daily Report, Central Eurasia,* FBIS-SOV-94-128, July 5, 1994, pp. 26–27.

8. "Chemical Weapons Threaten Volga Region. Deadline for Their Destruction May Not Be Met," *Izvestiya* (Moscow), February 18, 1994, pp. 1–2, translated in JPRS, *JPRS Report, Environmental Issues,* JPRS-TEN-94-007, March 15, 1994, pp. 32–33.

9. S. Leskov, "Plague and the Bomb: Russian and U.S. Military Bacteriological Programs Are Being Developed in Deep Secrecy and Present a Terrible Danger to the World," *Izvestiya* (Moscow), June 26, 1993.

10. For additional information dealing with the potential threat of nuclear theft see Chapter 1. Also see Cochran and Norris, *Russian/Soviet Nuclear Warhead Production*; William C. Potter, *Nuclear Profiles of the Soviet Successor States*, Monterey Institute of International Studies, monograph no. 1, Program for Nonproliferation Studies, Monterey, Calif., May 1993.

CHAPTER 6

1. The Medical Academy's Sysin Scientific Research Institute on Man and Hygiene of the Environment is cited as the source of this evaluation in the *State Report on the State of the Environment of the Russian Federation in 1992*, Moscow, 1993.

2. The cities identified were: Angarsk, Arkhangel'sk, Astrakhan', Barnaul, Berezniki, Bratsk, Bryansk, Chelyabinsk, Cherepovets, Groznyy, Gubacha, Kaliningrad, Kamensk-Ural'sky, Kemerovo, Khabarovsk, Krasnodar, Lipetsk, Magnitogorsk, Mednogorsk, Moscow, Nikel', Nizhniy Tagil, Noril'sk, Novocherkassk, Novokuznetsk, Novokuibishevek, Novomoskovsk, Omsk, Orsk, Perm', Prokopiyevsk, Salavat, Samara, Saratov, Shelekov, Sterlitamak, Togliatti, Volgograd, Yuzhno-Sakhalinsk, Yekaterinburg, Zapolyarnyy, and Zima. I am grateful to the World Bank for bringing to my attention Government Resolution N93 of 1993.

3. *State Report on the State of the Environment.*

4. Interview with Andrey Demin by Svetlana Sukhaya, "Don't Be Afraid of Mirrors: Russians Must Know the Truth about the Nation's Health," *Trud* (Moscow), April 1, 1994, p. 3, translated in Joint Publications Research Service, *JPRS Report, Environmental Issues*, JPRS-TEN-94-012, May 10, 1994, pp. 43–44.

5. Sergey Kudryashov, "Bashkiriya Hushes Up Ecological Problems," *Izvestiya* (Moscow), August 31, 1993. p. 2, translated in JPRS, *JPRS Report, Environmental Issues*, JPRS-TEN-93-026, November 24, 1993, pp. 49–50.

6. Interview with Sergey Myagov, chairman of the Coordinating Council on Unfavorable and Dangerous Natural Phenomena and Protection against Them, by Aleksandr Yuryev, "An Atlas of Catastrophes," *Delovoy mir* (Moscow), August 10, 1991, p. 12, translated in JPRS, *JPRS Report, Environmental Issues*, JPRS-TEN-91-019, November 15, 1991, pp. 60–61.

7. Andrey Bayduzhiy, "The End of the Century Will Be a Time of Catastrophes in Russia," *Nezavisimaya gazeta* (Moscow), July 7, 1993, p. 6, translated in Foreign Broadcast Information Service, *FBIS Report, Central Eurasia*, FBIS-USR-93-098, July 30, 1993, pp. 35–37.

8. Agence France Presse, Moscow, May 5, 1994; Radio Free Europe/Radio Liberty B-Wire, May 5, 1994.

9. V. Lipin, "Ekologicheskiy tupik? Khimiya prestupleniy," *SEA Bulletin*, no. 62–63 (June 11, 1993): 5–6.

10. I am indebted to Gregory Guroff for this quotation from his travels accompanying the senators and congressman.

11. D. Khrushchov et al., "Keeping Toxic Wastes from Sinking into the Sea," *Zelenyy svit* (Kiev), no. 5 (April 1994): 3, translated in FBIS, *FBIS Daily Report, Central Eurasia*, FBIS-USR-94-054, May 23, 1994, pp. 46–47.

12. Svetlana Stepunina, "Vladimir Karasev, Responsible Secretary of the Russian Federation President's Council for Ecological Policy: And the Committee for Emergency Situations Will Become the Country's Leading Ministry . . . " *Rossiyskiye vesti* (Moscow), June 4, 1993, pp. 3–4, translated in FBIS, *FBIS Daily Report, Central Eurasia*, FBIS-USR-93-076, June 21, 1993, pp. 38–41.

13. Ibid., p. 38.

14. Ibid.

15. In author's conversation (Washington, D.C., August 1994) with a leading physician and researcher from Ufa, it was indicated that no less than 90 percent of enterprises in the city involved military-related production.

16. Bayduzhiy, "The End of the Century Will Be a Time of Catastrophes in Russia," pp. 35–37.

17. Ibid.

18. Stepunina, "Vladimir Karasev."

19. Murray Feshbach, "Oil, Gas and the Environment in the Former Soviet Union," technical report to the United Nations' Division of Transnational Corporations and Management for the Working Group for Environmentally Sound Development of Oil and Gas in Russia, Vienna, August 1992.

20. V. P. Vorfolomeyev, "Ekologicheskaya bezopasnost' segodnya—s uchetom ekonomicheskikh realiy" ("Ecological Security Today—Taking into Account Economic Realities"), *Zelenyy mir* (Moscow), February 1, 1993, p. 4.

21. Radio Free Europe/Radio Liberty B-Wire, March 16, 1994.

22. Vorfolomeyev, "Ekologicheskaya bezopasnost' segodnya."

23. Letter signed by V. A. Durasov, V. A. Kryuchkov, and Y. A. Osipyan, addressed to President Gorbachev and entitled "O probleme zagryazneniya okruzhayushchey sredy v SSSR dioksinami," in accordance with USSR Presidential Order number 74355, dated December 21, 1989. In 1987, according to Yuri Izrael, almost 127 tons of benzo(a)pyrene were produced in the former Soviet Union. Benzo(a)pyrene usually is coproduced with dioxin as a by-product of less-than-optimal fossil fuel burning. The distribution of its sources was: ferrous and nonferrous metallurgy—50.8 tons (40 percent); chemical industry—20.3 tons (16 percent); machine building—11.4 tons (9 percent); fuel and energy sector—3.8 tons (3 percent); other types of industry—5.1 tons (4 percent); transport—2.5 tons (2 percent); and household heating—33.0 tons (26 percent). To the extent that this "production" gets into the ambient air, land, and water, it contributes significantly to the environmental problems of the country. See Yuri Izrael et al., "K probleme zagryazneniya prirodnoy sredy

benz(a)pirenom," *Meteorologiya i gidrologiya* (Moscow), no. 9 (September 1992): 38. In the United States and the former German Federal Republic, the maximum permissible levels of dioxin were between 1 and 5 mkg/kg; in Russia, levels of 10 to 140 mkg/kg were recorded in the twenty-nine cities cited by Lev Fyedorov as having significant medical problems. See Lev Fyedorov, "The Dioxin Expanse of the Former USSR: Its System of Coordinates Is Built on Secrecy, Lies and Incompetence," *Nezavisimaya gazeta* (Moscow), January 16, 1992, p. 6, translated in JPRS, *JPRS Report, Environmental Issues*, JPRS-TEN-92-009, May 22, 1992, pp. 68–70. Also see L. Fyedorov, *Dioksiny kak eko-logicheskaya opasnost': retrospektiva i perspektivy* (Moscow: Nauka, 1993).

24. Kudryashov, "Bashkiriya Hushes Up Ecological Problems."

25. Keith Schneider, "Fetal Harm Is Cited as Primary Hazard in Dioxin Exposure," *New York Times*, May 11, 1994, pp. A1, 20.

26. Fedor Orlov, "Leading the Whole Planet—Tens of Thousands of Pesticides: Lots, Even for a Big Country," *Segodnya* (Moscow), March 10, 1994, p. 9, translated in JPRS, *JPRS Report, Environmental Issues*, JPRS-TEN-94-010, April 15, 1994, pp. 21–22.

27. Ibid.

28. Orlov, "Leading the Whole Planet."

29. M. Karlov, "So Who Exactly Is Poisoning Us?" *Selskaya zhizn'* (Moscow), February 22, 1994, p. 1, translated in JPRS, *JPRS Report, Environmental Issues*, JPRS-TEN-94-007, March 15, 1994, p. 30.

30. Orlov, "Leading the Whole Planet."

31. A. Panov and W. Preobrazhenska, "Be Careful—Don't Eat 'Kovboy!'" *Zelenyy svit* (Kiev), no. 5 (April 1994): 4, translated in FBIS, *FBIS Report, Central Eurasia*, FBIS-USR-94-054, May 23, 1994, pp. 45–46.

32. Paul Brown, "Pesticides Kill 40,000 a Year Says UN Expert," *Guardian* (Manchester), April 26, 1994, p. 8. The figure of 40,000 people killed annually comes from a statement by Jan Huismans of the United Nations Environment Programme (UNEP).

33. "Missile Fuel Leaks Will Spell 'Catastrophe,'" *Nezavisimaya gazeta* (Moscow), March 25, 1992, pp. 1, 2. The chemical formula for heptyl is $[(CH_3)_2NNH_2]$.

34. Ibid.

35. Vladimir Karasev, "The Defense Industry Is Destroying the Natural World, But Can Help It Too," *Rossiyskiye vesti* (Moscow), March 19, 1993, pp. 3, 4, translated in JPRS, *JPRS Report, Environmental Issues*, JPRS-TEN-93-010, April 20, 1993, pp. 23–25. Karasev is the responsible secretary of the Ecological Policy Council under the president of the Russian Federation.

36. "Vesti" newscast, Russian Television Network (Moscow), May 2, 1994, translated in FBIS, *FBIS Daily Report, Central Eurasia*, FBIS-SOV-94-085, May 3, 1994, p. 24.

37. Menslu Jumbatova, cited in Vitali Chelishev, "Echo of a Silent Cry," paper prepared for a conference on Environment for Europe, Lucerne, April 28–30, 1993, pp. 2–3.

38. Thomas B. Cochran et al., *Soviet Nuclear Weapons*, Nuclear Weapons Databook, vol. 4, issued by the Natural Resources Defense Council, Inc., New York, 1989, p. 55.

39. Murray Feshbach, "The Toxic Archipelago," *Washington Post*, July 11, 1993, pp. C1, 4.

40. Vladimir Lupandin, "'Zheltyye deti,'" *Poisk* (Moscow), April 9–15, 1993, p. 6. Lupandin is also on the staff of the Russian Academy of Sciences' Institute of Sociology.

41. Murray Feshbach, "The Soviet Union Is Turning Its Land into a Desert," *Wall Street Journal*, May 17, 1992, p. A12, translated into Russian in *Izvestiya* (Moscow), May 18, 1992, p. 7.

42. Ministry of Environmental Protection and Natural Resources of the Russian Federation, *State of the Environmental and Conservation Activity in the Territory of the Former USSR: From Stockholm to Rio*, Moscow, 1994, p. 67.

43. Andrey Bayduzhiy, "Live Merchandise Leaving Russia. If Barriers Are Not Placed on Its Path, the Red Book Could Turn into Many Volumes," *Nezavisimaya gazeta* (Moscow), January 11, 1994, p. 6, translated in JPRS, *JPRS Report, Environmental Issues*, JPRS-TEN-94-003, February 7, 1994, pp. 30–31. According to Bayduzhiy, the actual volume of trade may be more than ten times greater than registered by official permits. Russia now coordinates permits for such animal and plant species for Ukraine, Belarus, Kazakhstan, Kyrgyzstan, Tajikistan, Turkmenistan, and Uzbekistan.

44. Ministry of Ecology and Administration of the President of the Russian Federation, *Gosudarstvennyy doklad o sostoyanii prirodnoy okruzhayushchey prirodnoy sredy Rossiyskoy Federatsii v 1992 godu*, Moscow, 1993.

45. K. Smirnov, "The Most Frightening Predator—the Poacher," *Izvestiya* (Moscow), April 7, 1993, p. 6.

46. "The Hunters Are Not Playing on Equal Terms with the Wolves," *Moskovskiye novosti* (Moscow), no. 9, (February 9, 1993): 5A, translated in JPRS, *JPRS Report, Enviromental Issues*, JPRS-TEN-93-010, April 20, 1993, p. 21.

47. The Golitsyn report was prepared in July 1992 for Radio Free Europe/Radio Liberty. It was entitled "Ecological Problems in the CIS during the Transitional Period," *RFE/RL Research Report* vol. 2, no. 2 (January 8, 1993): 37.

48. Ministry of Ecology and Administration of the President of the Russian Federation, *Gosudarstvennyy doklad o sostoyanii okruzhayushchey prirodnoy sredy Rossiyskoy Federatsii v 1991 godu*, Moscow, 1992, p. 50.

CHAPTER 7

1. Briefing for Under Secretary of State for Global Issues Timothy Wirth and staff, U.S. Department of State, May 19, 1994.

2. Unofficially, it has been estimated that some 30 to 40 percent of output is not captured by the official statistical systems. Therefore, the official

production decline is overstated but still serious. The production decline is more noticeable for goods than services.

3. Frederick Kempe, *Siberian Odyssey: A Voyage into the Russian Soul* (New York: G. P. Putnam's Sons, 1992), p. 60.

4. Clay Chandler, "The World Bank Turns 50, and Promises Some Changes," *Washington Post*, July 20, 1994, pp. F1–2.

5. "Their Dollars for Our Environment," *Rossiyskaya gazeta* (Moscow), June 10, 1994, p. 3, translated in Joint Publications Research Service, *JPRS Report, Environmental Issues*, JPRS-TEN-94-017, June 30, 1994, pp. 33–34.

6. One of the initial problems faced by Western planners in Indonesia in the early 1970s, similar to that faced by Western planners in the FSU today, was the unreliability of basic data and the difficulty in achieving a consensus on the most important economic realities. By synchronizing the publication of annual reports, the IGGI achieved an important step toward forcing all Western aid organizations to develop a common economic data base.

7. Paul Lewis, "Rich Nations Plan $2 Billion for Environment," *New York Times*, March 17, 1994, p. A 7.

8. Interfax (Moscow), June 15, 1994, transcribed in Foreign Broadcast Information Service, *FBIS Daily Report, Central Eurasia*, FBIS-SOV-94-116, June 16, 1994, p. 35.

9. "Vesti" newscast, Russian Television Network (Moscow), April 26, 1992, translated in FBIS, *FBIS Daily Report, Central Eurasia*, FBIS-SOV-92-083, April 29, 1992, p. 6.

10. The chief public relations officer of the Russian state nuclear concern, Rosenergoatom, told Interfax in April 1994 that Western insistence on closing Chernobyl-type nuclear reactors was a result of foreign concerns seeking to force their own nuclear plant design on Russia. "Russian Nuclear Concern Says Chernobyl-Type Reactors Are O.K.," Radio Free Europe/Radio Liberty *Daily Report*, April 29, 1994.

11. Valeriy Menshikov, et al., "Nuclear Power Engineering: Can We Expect Disasters or Advantages?" *Izvestiya* (Moscow), August 28, 1993, p. 4, translated in FBIS, *FBIS Report, Central Eurasia*, FBIS-USR-93-127, October 1, 1993, pp. 67–69.

12. Steven Mufson, "G-7 Eyes Aid for Ex-Soviet Nuclear Plants," *Washington Post*, May 22, 1992, pp. F1, 3.

13. Aleksandr Litvinov, ITAR-TASS (Moscow), May 5, 1994, transcribed in FBIS, *FBIS Daily Report, Central Eurasia*, FBIS-SOV-94-088, May 6, 1994, p. 35.

14. UT-1 Television Network (Kiev), May 5, 1994, translated in FBIS, *FBIS Daily Report, Central Eurasia*, FBIS-SOV-94-088, May 6, 1994, p. 35.

15. Paul Lewis, "New Proposal for Shutdown at Chernobyl," *New York Times*, July 3, 1994, p. 9.

16. Yuriy Arkhipov, Radio Rossii Network (Moscow), June 8, 1993, translated in FBIS, *FBIS Daily Report, Central Eurasia*, FBIS-SOV-93-109,

June 9, 1993, p. 20. Also, see *Pravda* (Moscow), June 8, 1993, p. 1, for more details.

17. Marat Zubko, "Finns Help Kola Nuclear Power Station," *Izvestiya* (Moscow), March 30, 1993, p. 3, translated in JPRS, *JPRS Report, Environmental Issues*, JPRS-TEN-93-009, April 9, 1993, pp. 24–25.

18. Bjorn Lindahl, "Russian Nuclear Waste Worries Norway," *Svenska Dagbladet* (Stockholm), April 18, 1994, p. 7, translated in JPRS, *JPRS Report, Environmental Issues*, JPRS-TEN-94-012, May 10, 1994, pp. 32–33.

19. Interfax (Moscow), January 29, 1993.

20. NCA/Agence France Presse, "Japan, Russia Agree to Build Nuke Waste Plant," Radio Free Europe/Radio Liberty A-Wire, April 29, 1994, 20:47:01 (CNO115).

21. See *Baltic Eco News* (Stockholm), no. 1 (January 1992): 4–6, for a listing of the first round of Baltic Eco Projects and a description of their goals.

22. Lotta Forsman, "Small Scale Projects Will Clean the Baltic Sea," in ibid., p. 7.

23. "Crusaders Making Waves in an Ocean of Pollution: The Baltic Is an Open Sewer, but Little Is Done to Clean It Up," *The European* (London), September 9–12, 1993, p. 4.

24. Interview with Russian Federation Ministry of Defense Ecology and Special Protection Systems Directorate chief Colonel Sergey Ivanovich Grigorov by Ivan Sas, Ministry of Defense press service associate, "Colonel Sergey Grigorov: 'Society Can Count on the Army During Ecological Cataclysms,'" *Krasnaya zvezda* (Moscow), December 18, 1992, p. 1, translated in JPRS, *JPRS Report, Environmental Issues*, JPRS-TEN-93-003, February 16, 1993, pp. 36–37.

25. See Murray Feshbach, unpublished report on "Soviet Military Health Problems," Georgetown University, 1990.

26. Viktor Litovkin, "Ecological Defenders Have Appeared in the Russian Army," *Izvestiya* (Moscow), June 17, 1993, p. 6, translated in JPRS, *JPRS Report, Environmental Issues*, JPRS-TEN-93-021, August 23, 1993, p. 21.

27. Radio Rossii Network (Moscow), August 3, 1993, translated in JPRS, *JPRS Report, Environmental Issues*, JPRS-TEN-93-022, September 3, 1993, p. 12.

28. Cf. *Voyennyy vestnik* (Moscow), no. 2 (February 1993): C4.

29. Vladimir Karasev, "Earth: A View From Space. On Cooperation Between Russia and the United States in the Area of Ecological Monitoring," *Rossiyskiye vesti* (Moscow) September 24, 1993, p. 11, translated in JPRS, *JPRS Report, Environmental Issues*, JPRS-TEN-93-026, November 24, 1993, pp. 50–51. Karasev is secretary of the Ecological Policy Council under the president of the Russian Federation.

30. This list, which is incomplete, is based on published Russian and Western sources.

31. See Thomas B. Cochran and Robert Standish Norris, *Russian/Soviet Nuclear Warhead Production*, Nuclear Weapons Databook, working papers, issued by the NRDC, September 8, 1993; and Murray Feshbach, "The Toxic Archipelago," *Washington Post*, July 11, 1993, pp. C1, 4.

32. Fred Hiatt, "Trying to Save Lake Baikal's Treasures—on a Salary of $13 a Month," *Washington Post*, May 31, 1994, p. A14.

33. In many ways the project, which will be undertaken by the U.S. Environmental Protection Agency Office of Air Quality Planning and Standards to clean up the air pollution problems at Volgograd, should be considered a model of a proper pilot project. While Volgograd is not the most polluted city in Russia, it has a number of features that make it a good choice for a demonstration project, including progressive local leadership, local industries that are seeking joint ventures, accessibility, and local environmental support.

34. The principal Western contribution—vaccines and syringes/needles—should be relatively inexpensive. *The Looming Crisis of Children and Women in Kyrgyzstan*, report of a UNICEF/WHO collaborative mission with the participation of the United Nations Development Programme, the United Nations Fund for Population Activities, and the World Food Program, February 21–26, 1992, estimated that it costs about $40,000 per million population to supply vaccines for measles, polio, BCG, DPT plus one-time syringes and needles for Kyrgyzstan. Assuming a total target population for the FSU of 80 million needing these vaccines and supplies, a rough estimate of costs would be less than $3.5 million. The bulk of the cost would depend on the level of Western personnel involvement in-country for purposes of visibility and program quality control. The Kyrgyz report is one of many prepared for the CIS countries. It is used here as a model rather than citing each and every country report.

35. Ibid.

36. These program cost estimates also are based on the UNICEF/WHO study of the health crisis in Kyrgyzstan. UNICEF/WHO estimates a total cost of $219,487 per one million population for the highest-priority drugs and supplies (but not including vaccines, needles, etc.). Assuming a target population of 12 million (1987 Soviet data) for Russia, total program cost should be approximately $2.6 million. The additional cost is based on the assumption that use of in-country medical personal would be desirable.

37. See the December 1992 and June/July 1994 issues of *CommonHealth* for the listing of AIHA health-care partnerships, also listed in Appendix D.

38. This study recommends that all proposed programs be phased in over a number of years in order to build up experience and reduce mistakes, and most importantly to ensure ongoing local institutional support.

39. From a number of exchanges with environmental experts at the World Bank, the author has been given to understand that the Bank is also now thinking that its major environmental effort, particularly in the area of water pollution abatement, should be in the area of technical assistance to create an adequate legal and regulatory framework and to strengthen environmental and natural resource management, policy formulation, and institutional capabilities at the federal, regional, and local levels.

40. Michael Specter, "Kola Peninsula in Russian Arctic May Be Pollution Capital of the World," *New York Times*, March 28, 1994, p. A1.

41. Interview with Andrey Demin by Svetlana Sukhaya, "Don't Be Afraid of Mirrors: Russians Must Know the Truth about the Nation's Health," *Trud* (Moscow), April 1, 1994, p. 3, translated in JPRS, *JPRS Report, Environmental Issues*, JPRS-TEN-94-012, May 10, 1994, pp. 43–44.

42. "Draft Concept of Russian Federation Environmental Security," *Zelenyy mir* (Moscow), no. 1 (January 1994): 6–9, translated in JPRS, *JPRS Report, Environmental Issues*, JPRS-TEN-94-015, June 9, 1994, pp. 30–39, especially pp. 37–38.

43. Again, this should be a multiyear program with a requirement that there be matching funds (at some level) from the receiving government. Here again, considerable savings could be achieved by procuring slightly older equipment. The ratio of equipment to training funding should be about two to one.

44. The U.S. contribution should be heavily focused on the creation of this television program and should phase down considerably once the project is launched, for both program and political reasons.

45. Alternatively, the author has proposed the formation of a Center for Post-Soviet Environmental Security Studies to be based at Georgetown University. Scholarly and policy-related research in conjunction with Yablokov's Center for Ecological Policy and the World Laboratory Data Bank of Dr. Grigoriy Barenboim will be conducted. In addition NGOs, like the Center for Independent Ecological Programs, will be crucial partners of the Center.

46. Letter prepared by Maria V. Cherkasova, head of the CIEP.

AFTERWORD

1. Interview with Frederic Hauge, head of research, the Bellona Foundation at Georgetown University, Washington, D.C., July 7, 1994. He has been to specific potential and/or actual pollution sites more than sixty times.

INDEX

ABOUT THE AUTHOR

Murray Feshbach is research professor of demography at Georgetown University. He has served as chief of the U.S.S.R. Population, Employment, and Research and Development branch of the Foreign Demographic Analysis division of the U.S. Bureau of the Census. At the request of the U.S. Department of State he served as the first Sovietologist-in-residence in the Office of the Secretary-General of NATO, Lord Carrington. He has been a fellow of the Kennan Institute of the Woodrow Wilson International Center for Scholars, Smithsonian Institution, and is past president of the American Association for the Advancement of Slavic Studies and the Association for Comparative Economic Studies, a member of the Council on Foreign Relations and of the International Institute of Strategic Studies. He is coauthor of *Ecocide in the U.S.S.R.: Health and Nature under Siege* (with Alfred Friendly, Jr.) and is chief editor of an *Environmental and Health Atlas of Russia*, to be published in Russian and in English in March 1995.

The Twentieth Century Fund sponsors and supervises timely analyses of economic policy, foreign affairs, and domestic political issues. Not-for-profit and nonpartisan, the Fund was founded in 1919 and endowed by Edward A. Filene.

The Twentieth Century Fund Press
41 East 70th Street, NY, NY 10021

To order, call 1 (800) 275-1447

ISBN 0-87078-364-5

50995

9 780870 783647

Twentieth Century Fund